401

The Extraordinary Story of the Man who
Ran 401 Marathons in 401 Days and
Changed his Life Forever

Ben Smith

BLOOMSBURY SPORT
LONDON • OXFORD • NEW YORK • NEW DELHI • SYDNEY

For Kyle

And the thousands of people that made The 401 Challenge the success it was, you know who you are.

BLOOMSBURY SPORT
Bloomsbury Publishing Plc

50 Bedford Square, London, WC1B 3DP, UK

BLOOMSBURY, BLOOMSBURY SPORT and the Diana logo are trademarks of
Bloomsbury Publishing Plc

First published in Great Britain 2018

A catalogue record for this book is available from the British Library
Library of Congress Cataloguing-in-Publication data has been applied for

ISBN: Trade paperback: 978-1-4729-5618-7; eBook: 978-1-4729-5619-4

2 4 6 8 10 9 7 5 3 1

Typeset in Minion Pro by Deanta Global Publishing Services, Chennai, India
Printed and bound in the UK by CPI Group (UK) Ltd, Croydon, CR0 4YY

To find out more about our authors and books visit www.bloomsbury.com
and sign up for our newsletters

Contents

Over the years, I've met lots of people doing crazy, ambitious challenges. Many of them have remarkable, often heartbreaking, stories to tell. Most of them are genuine people, and I try to support them as much as I can, but I usually see them once and never again. Not Ben. From the moment I met him, I knew there was something special about him. It wasn't just what he was doing – although completing 401 marathons in 401 days is obviously remarkable in itself – it was also how he was doing it. It was his incredible charisma. It was the smile that never seemed to leave his face. It was his extraordinary enthusiasm and energy. I loved that he stopped off for coffee and cake every day. I loved that he got people off their sofas and running. Most of all, I loved that he'd had the courage to change his life and step into the unknown.

When I first heard about Ben and The 401 Challenge, I did think he was slightly mad. What he was trying to do was way out there, beyond anything I'd heard about. But I always thought he'd do it. On the first day I met him, I was lucky enough to watch him tell his story to a roomful of teenage kids, and it came straight from the heart. I like that about Ben: what you see is what you get. He spoke about how he was bullied at school, how he had tried to take his own life. But the main message I took away from that talk was to be yourself, do what you want to do, and not what others think you should do. It sounds like a simple message, but his story has so many layers to it, which is why Ben inspires so many people for so many different reasons. Doing 401 marathons in 401 days could be pretty boring, but Ben brought so much more to it.

People tell me all the time: 'I used to run against you, back in the day.' I must have heard that line a thousand times. At some point, they stopped running and started doing other things. People so easily end up doing things in life they don't want to do, and then, 10 or 20 years down the line, they think to themselves: 'How on earth did I end up here? This isn't what I wanted to do with my life.' In Ben, I recognised somebody who saw that his life wasn't going the way he wanted it to, and was brave enough and strong enough to alter its direction – 'Hang on a minute, there are other things I want to do, and other things I need to do.' That's why we hit it off and remain such good friends. His is a great story, and one I like to share with as many people as possible.

Steve Cram, former 1500m world champion and 1500m and mile world record holder

I remember being told about The 401 Challenge and thinking: 'This guy is a complete nutter.' Then I got to know him and why he was doing it. He was such an unassuming, modest person, but I could feel his inner strength. Just running 401 marathons is really inspirational, but the fact that he was such a genuine and normal guy made his story that much stronger.

I did have misgivings about him running 401 marathons in 401 days, but I think he did, too. The Challenge was obviously going to be physically tough. Elite athletes just couldn't get their heads around doing seven marathons in a week, let alone what he was trying to do. My peak mileage was 151 miles in a week, and he was doing more than 180 miles in a week, for 57 weeks in a row. So I did think his body was going to fall apart. And, in fairness, it did. But I also thought the mental side would be tougher. Day 401 must seem a long, long way off when you've 'only' done 99 marathons, or 150, or 200. Or one! But because of his extraordinary mental strength and focus, he was able to shrug that off, get out there, day after day, and hold it all together.

So many people end up on a path they don't really want to be on, but they haven't got the strength and courage to turn back and try another way instead. But he taught people that it's never too late to completely change your life around and be the person you really want to be. And he's motivated so many kids and adults who have been bullied to re-build their self-confidence, and therefore their lives. Ben's story has helped so many people, but he doesn't think he is special, which is what is so special about him. I love that I got to meet him. I admire him so much.

Paula Radcliffe, marathon world record holder

Nothing Special

My footsteps are soft drumbeats on the sand, easing my body back into a rhythm. And every step I take, I discover another piece of myself. I know it sounds clichéd, but not as clichéd as the drudgery of my old existence: a job that was draining my soul, big bucks, big house, big car, pension plan, two holidays a year I was too stressed to enjoy. In other words, what success is supposed to look like and therefore how most people choose to live.

Life is a series of choices, which is not what everybody wants to hear, because it reminds them they are ultimately responsible for their own contentment. They wake up every morning, commute to the office, come home, sit in front of the TV – because they are too mentally drained to think of an alternative and enjoy all the other things they have worked so hard to buy – and repeat, *ad nauseam*. And all the while they're hoping for something more. I know, because this was my life – feeling trapped, groaning inside, conforming to what I thought society deemed to be success. But here I am, cresting a dune on a beach in Northumberland – Holy Island stretched out in front of me, Bamburgh Castle to my left, sun directly above me, not a soul in sight to share the view with. I take a seat and think: 'Obviously this was meant to be – just me, on a deserted beach, taking everything in, exactly at this moment.' Maybe, maybe not. I'd hate to think we live in a world where there's no element of control. I don't believe our lives are mapped out for us, but it's our choices which ultimately put us on the paths we end up following. And it's the paths we follow which dictate our landscapes. People sometimes say to me: 'I can't do what you did. It's easier said than done, it's not that simple.' But it *is* that simple, which isn't the same as saying it's not hard. Running is just putting one foot in front of the other – that's the simple bit – the hard part is choosing to go running in the first place. But once you make that choice, you can start putting distance between your old life and closing in on a new one.

Running was the thing I found that made me truly happy, and it works nicely as a metaphor – freedom, taking steps, leaving things behind – but it can be anything. Everybody has something inside them that will make them happy, and in my opinion you just need to find out what that is. And when you find out, you'll see that security isn't the same as happiness. But because we've become so programmed to believe that happiness is quantified by the materialistic stuff we have – and because the head so often rules the heart – too many people think they're happy when they're not, so they don't even bother looking for it. It's like that old quote says: lots of people die with their song still inside them. Even choosing to look takes guts – it's one thing discovering what makes you happy, another following it through, because that can lead to taking risks. And risk-taking isn't for everybody. Dare I say it, neither is happiness.

I look at my wrist – exactly 5000 miles on the clock. That's a long way from my old existence, but it all started with a single step. Time to go back to work, I've still got 5506 miles to go. But I'm not going to sit around and moan about it. One foot in front of the other, soft drumbeats on the sand, easing my body back into that rhythm again, thinking: 'No possessions, no money, no idea where the next wage is coming from, all ties severed from my old life. But I'm not worried, I'll find something, what will be, will be…' Some people might call it drifting, but the smile on my face says it's an exciting way to live.

There's something you should know from the outset: that job that was draining my soul, the big bucks, the big house, the big car, the pension plan, the two holidays a year – that was one of the best parts of my life before now, my world after I'd been 'fixed'. I was 16 and a half stone, smoked 20–30 cigarettes a day, had a mini-stroke at 29. Oh, and I was married to a woman, even though I knew I was gay. And everything was supposed to be right with the world! Mad, isn't it? The part before that was the actual bad part. It doesn't even feel like my life anymore – I filed it away, often while running. But it's important that I have a rummage around and show you just how broken I was; to show you that – you know what? – life can be pretty shit, but you can climb out of it. It takes blood, sweat and tears, but I no longer believe anything is impossible. You don't have to run 401 marathons in a row, like I chose to do, but you do have to start by putting one foot in front of the other and take it from there. I'm a normal guy, nothing special. And that's the point.

CHAPTER 1

Broken

There are only so many times you can fix yourself. You break, you patch yourself up. You break again, you patch yourself up again. But there comes a point when you've been broken so many times, there is nothing left to patch up. If a car keeps breaking, eventually you take it away to be scrapped. And that's exactly how I felt – utterly worthless and ready for the scrap heap.

It was a Sunday, the school was quiet, the half-boarders having gone home for the weekend, and a storm was brewing outside. I went down for dinner, took a knife from the cutlery drawer, put it in my pocket, walked down the long corridor of the school and back upstairs to my boarding house room. From that point on, I remember what I think I remember, but I honestly don't know if it's real, because it was as if I was in a trance. Sitting on my bed, I can see where I was in relation to my window, and where the desk was in relation to my door. But one thing I know for certain: I had every intention of taking my own life. This wasn't a cry for help, it was desperation, a feeling of wanting to end it all. I had made the decision I was going to take back control. I'd got to a point where I couldn't handle anything anymore and could no longer see a way out. I was sad, lonely, lost and isolated. I'd been broken so many times, I was almost psychotic. I got up, tidied my room, made my bed, lay on it and started to cry. But even though I was crying, I wasn't really emotional, strange as that might sound, because all the emotion had been kicked out of me. Then I picked up the knife and started cutting at my wrists. I cut crosswise, so maybe, albeit subconsciously, I knew it wasn't going to work.

There was a knock at the door and I suddenly became worried that somebody might see me. I looked down at my wrists – there was blood, but not enough to end things or require an admission to hospital. So I got up, went to the door and unlocked it, peered out into the corridor but nobody was there. I thought to myself: 'Now what do I do?' I'd plucked up the courage to kill myself and it hadn't worked, and now I wasn't brave enough to give it another shot. I shut the door, slid down it, slumped to the floor and burst into tears. And now I was angry: I didn't even have the balls to do the one thing that would have given me back control of my own life. And then even the crying stopped. There's only so much crying you can do. I was left feeling empty, ashamed and sick to the core.

. . . .

I can't remember the first time I was bullied, but I know it started just after I arrived at boarding school. I was 10 and suddenly transplanted from a loving and supportive family into this cold, frightening building in the middle of nowhere, crammed with kids who, in my opinion, had been dumped there by their parents. Mum and Dad didn't want to send me to boarding school – that wasn't how they worked because we were a very close family. To this day I don't really know why I had to be sent to that place, but one thing I've learned is that choices need to be made. Sometimes they're right and sometimes they're not. Dad was in the Royal Air Force, meaning we moved around a lot. I was born in Wendover, Buckinghamshire, and spent a couple of years in Scotland, before the family moved to Visselhoevede, a village between Hannover and Hamburg in Germany, where my brother Dan was born. I loved my childhood. We were the only English family in the village, the locals welcomed us with open arms and it was an idyllic time. I was an outgoing kid, with a real sense of adventure, and because I moved around a lot and got to meet lots of different people, I found it easy to make friends. Back then, Dan and I got on like a house on fire. We were inseparable, even to the extent that if I was offered something, I'd always say: 'Can my brother have one as well, please?'

After Visselhoevede, we moved to Norwich for a couple of years before Dad was posted to the NATO base in Ramstein, back in Germany. But because there was no British school, my parents had no choice but to send me to boarding school back in England. I flew to England with Mum and Dad. Both of them and Grandma took me to look at a couple of schools. One was horrific – if you were unwell, you had to drag your mattress out of your bedroom and stick it in the sick room. I remember cowering behind Mum, shaking my head and saying, 'I don't want to go here!' So we chose the lesser of two evils. Mum bought me a new pencil case, I sat in on some lessons and came away thinking: 'I really enjoyed that, everyone was really nice to me.'

Because I'd grown up having adventures, I was open to new experiences but I didn't really grasp that I wouldn't be going home to Mum and Dad once lessons were over. So, when Mum left me there for the first time, lying on my bunk bed in the dark with a room full of strange kids, I remember thinking: 'This doesn't feel like home at all.' It was like I didn't belong there – I felt lost and abandoned and really scared.

The first time I was bullied my reaction was: 'Oh, why did they say that?' Before then my childhood might have been idyllic, but it was also very sheltered. Softly-spoken, sensitive and innocent, I was not your typical lad. I wasn't keen on football or rugby, which marked me out as 'different'. I was more interested in being nice to people and I didn't fight back, and that, of course, made me a very easy target. And because people didn't seem interested in being nice to me, I quickly became quite reclusive. On my 11th birthday, Mum and Dad sent me a load of toy cars. Soon I was obsessed with them – I took them out of their boxes, went behind the school and played with them on the path, I was just so happy. But it makes me sad thinking about it now as the other kids picked on me because of that. There was nobody to play with because the other kids were so much more mature than me and I was still so child-like. They were obviously better at adapting to the school environment, while I just wanted to be a kid.

There were times I just wanted attention, for somebody to hug me, tell me everything was going to be alright, and act like my parents would have done had they been there. Some of the teachers told me it would get better and I'd get stronger. Without actually saying it, they were telling me to man up. It wasn't within the school's culture to be sympathetic, the general attitude was: 'What are you complaining about, child?' At night, the only person around to talk to was a really creepy teacher who lived at the end of the corridor. He was like a character from a Roald Dahl story, with a Hitler-style moustache and bits and pieces of food stuck between his teeth. When you had a nightmare, you were supposed to knock on his door and wake him up. Because he terrified me so much, when I had nightmares I'd end up walking around the school in the dark. There was no comfort or compassion or empathy, it felt like prison to me.

The night before I was due to go back to school after a holiday, I wouldn't sleep. Mum would lie on my bed, stroke my hair and tell me everything was going to be alright. In the morning, I wouldn't eat anything because I felt so sick; I was wound up and crying. When it was time to leave, Dad would literally have to drag me from the house and into the car. I'd be kicking and screaming, clinging to the railings. It wasn't nice for me, I was so scared of going back, but it was also horrific for Mum to see her son like that. I can only imagine the pain and torture it caused her and Dad.

Back at the school those few sensitive teachers with any idea about pastoral care or empathy continued to be barked down by the majority. The nurse was lovely, and I'd fake headaches so I could take a soluble aspirin, sit in the sick room and escape from everything. In my final year, I was craving attention so much, wanting somebody to be compassionate towards me, that I squirted shower gel all over my bed, ripped up a picture of Mum and Dad, went to a teacher and said: 'Look what somebody has done!' Another kid saw me do it and confronted me, but I fought long and hard and insisted it wasn't me. Eventually, a teacher dragged me up in front of the whole school and said: 'Whoever did this, we will find out and they will be punished.' Obviously, they never did. I was so screwed-up! That same year, every pupil was named head of table for both dinner and lunch sittings, except me, which made me feel like an even bigger outcast. By the age of 12, any happiness had been squashed out of me and I was really fucked up.

．．．．．．．．．．

Beverley Smith, Ben's mum: *Ben wasn't cut out for boarding school and we knew it wasn't right for him. He was soft, gentle and caring. He was also outgoing when he felt safe, so he'd always been outgoing in the environment we brought him up in. He attracted all sorts of people and latched on to anyone that looked a little bit different. If there was a big girl, he'd pal up with her. If there was a black or Asian child, he'd make friends with them. He had Chinese friends, German, Portuguese, Russian, you name it. There were times when our back garden would be like the United Nations. He was so* trusting and didn't see any difference in anybody. But because he was so accepting of people, that characteristic attracted the bullies.

Ben's brother Daniel was hard on the outside but soft in the middle, whereas Ben was soft all over. When we lived in Norwich, Daniel played mini-rugby and loved it. The first time we took both of them to the rugby club, I said to them: 'You don't have to do this, you can just watch if you want.' Daniel was off like a shot, Ben hid behind my legs. But after a while, Ben said: 'Actually, I might like to have a try.' So off came the tracksuit and on he went. Ten minutes went by and I began to think: 'Where has Ben gone?' All the other kids were down one end of the field and Ben was at the other, making daisy chains. It was typical Ben, the sensitive soul. That was probably down to his grandma – she was always wandering around a lake, near her flat, with the boys, picking flowers. He was so innocent, probably too innocent. And he was also naïve because we were naïve. I wasn't what they would call streetwise, I trusted everybody. If I got a good kicking, I went back for another because I'd think: 'They didn't just do that to me, surely?' It was Ben's naïvety the bullies preyed on and his innocence they took away.

We did ask the school about its level of pastoral care, things like: 'Do they get a cuddle if they need one?' Because we were a very tactile family, I used to sit with the boys and read them stories and stroke their hair. So we didn't expect what he got. We saw him as often as we could. There were times when we would suddenly up sticks and come over to the UK, and I'd feel like crying, watching all the other kids playing with each other. He was close to my mum and some weekends he'd stay with her in Rotherham and have a great time. And every *end of term he'd either come to Germany or we'd go down to my mum's. It was the three months in between that were the problem. I'd always go and collect him at the end of term or pick him up from the airport, but I could never do the other journey because I could see how unhappy he was. He'd be absolutely heartbroken, and so would I. Even now, it makes me cry, just thinking about it.*

. . . .

When it was time to go to secondary school at 13, I thought: 'I suppose this bullying's going to end now.' But at secondary school, things escalated quickly. The plan had been to pull me from school when Mum and Dad moved back to the UK. But then they got posted to Buchan, near Aberdeen, and they had heard the local kids didn't look too kindly on English kids from a military background. Things could have turned out far worse, which is a sobering thought. The abuse was now physical, which is not to say that the mental abuse stopped. I was dyslexic, not great at reading and writing, so kids would label me thick. And suddenly, lots of kids were calling me gay, a word I hadn't really heard before – 'You're gay! You're gay! You're gay!' I wouldn't say I was camp or effeminate, but I was quite shy and softly-spoken. I didn't really know what being gay was, but I thought it was a bad thing. At school we were in church almost every day, so I had this crazy idea that being gay was un-Godly, abnormal and unhuman.

Every morning, I'd wake up thinking: 'What's going to happen to me today?' One incident I remember to this day was when I was in the computer room, playing the game Doom. All the usual suspects were in there, ganging up on me, killing me in the game, relentlessly taunting me, calling me gay or weird or both. I grew angrier and angrier and more frustrated and eventually I lost it, completely flipped out, and punched one of them. I stood back and thought: 'Oh, shit, what have I done?' To save face, he chased me out of the computer room, through the corridor, up into my bedroom and beat seven bells of shit out of me on my bed. My bedroom was my only sanctuary, in what I had commonly come to refer to as 'hell on earth', and he invaded it. I was curled up in the foetal position, thinking, 'I just want this all to end', when someone else from my house walked in and had the balls to say: 'Whoa, what's going on here?' To this day I appreciate him doing that. It takes a strong kid to stand up for somebody else who's being bullied. But I felt weak not being able to fight back, and a little confused as to why. For many nights after the incident, I dreamt about what I would do if it happened again. I saw myself fighting the bully and winning, after a martial arts-style frenzy. It was completely absurd, but a way of dealing with the situation.

The mental bullying was worse because it wasn't intermittent, it was constant, like psychological warfare. It left a scar no one could see with the naked eye. I lived in constant fear, and that zaps your energy, your confidence, your everything. Maybe the kids were feeling abandoned and wanted to somehow regain control of their lives and the only way they felt they could do this was to abuse somebody else and make their life hell. Perhaps it was a case of wanting to belong. One of my bullies turned out to be gay, so maybe he hated himself and was taking it out on me? Whatever the reasons, it wasn't just kids being kids, that's just a cheap excuse. In my opinion kids are born as blank slates and it's their influences and experiences growing up that mould them into the people they become. That was certainly the case with me, so why would it be any different for my bullies? But what was going on in their lives that meant they had turned out like this?

There were a few bullies in particular who made my life a misery. After I left school, I'd search for the boys online, hoping they'd had a bad time of it and their lives had gone to shit. One had no online presence at all, so I never found out what happened to him. Another has a young family and sometimes I'd think: 'I'd like your kids to know how you treated me.' But then I'd think: 'Maybe these people just don't realise how nasty they were being, or maybe they don't even remember me?'

There's a lot I've blocked out from those days, but I do remember sitting in the phone box on the top floor of the house many times, sobbing down the line to Mum: 'Just come and get me, please come and get me...' But I didn't tell my parents what was going on, I kept it all to myself. They were obviously aware I was sad, but they didn't really know why, so had no concrete reason to remove me from the situation, which is what I wanted. I remember a throwaway comment from Mum: 'You know, this has almost broken me and your dad up.' That put a lot of responsibility on me. Actually, it led to me putting a lot of responsibility on myself. I didn't want them to know I was being bullied because I didn't want them to go through all that again. And if they'd broken up, I don't think I would have been able to forgive myself. So, every time I was asked if I was being bullied, I'd say: 'Everything is fine, I think I just feel a bit homesick...'

* * * * * * * * * *

Beverley Smith, Ben's mum: *Pete being in the Air Force, it was extremely difficult to make plans. You never knew where you'd be from one day to the next, and in those days, they told you where you were being posted, you weren't asked. We had* an inkling Ben was being bullied because he was clearly unhappy. 'What's the matter?' we used to say. And he'd say: 'I just miss home a bit.' The situation was the only thing that ever threatened our marriage. I was caught in the middle because Germany was the tour Pete had wanted all his working life. And he deserved it, he'd worked so hard for it. But it became such a strain that I thought about coming back to the UK. Pete was away a lot, so when Ben came home for holidays, I used to say to him: 'Daddy's away, so you're the man of the house now.' Little did I know that what seemed like just a harmless, throwaway comment sat on Ben's shoulders like a heavy weight. And because Ben was so sensitive, this comment was stored away and he lived his life thinking he must never let his Mum and Dad down.

The headmaster of the secondary school had visited the prep school and what struck a chord with Ben was when he said: 'Every child that comes here will have a fresh start.' So Ben decided that was the school for him. And because Daniel was jealous of what Ben had, and saw it as an adventure, he insisted he wanted to go, too.

In our naïvety we believed what the headmaster had said, but it turned out to be a load of crap. I told his housemaster that we thought Ben had been bullied at prep school and that he was quite a sensitive young man. But while we were in Scotland, we got a phone call from Ben, who was saying: 'They're chasing me and I've got nowhere else to go!' Pete kept talking to Ben, while I rang his housemaster and said: 'I don't know what's going on down there, but something is, because Ben has been on the phone, telling us he's being chased!'

We dropped everything in Scotland and when we finally arrived we discovered there was this particular group of lads who'd been teasing Ben and flinging all his gear about and what not. It might not sound like much, but because of the type of lad Ben was, and because of how much damage had already been done, he couldn't take it. There was also a big class divide because these bullies paid full school fees, whereas our kids were what they called 'military brats', which meant the Air Force paid part of their fees. So Ben and Daniel were natural targets. We used to say to them both: 'Talk to us, tell us what's wrong, you can come home.' But because Ben wouldn't communicate, we had no idea of what he was going through. It was always: 'I'm so sorry for worrying you, I'm so sorry for this, I'm so sorry for that.'

We had a word with his housemaster and he said: 'Oh, Mrs Smith, you're worrying too much, it's just boys being boys…' But it wasn't: the school was trying to cover up the bullying that was going on. Still Ben never said anything. Every time they came home, the pair of them would bring shadows with them. It would take them the whole weekend to unwind, and when the time came for us to take them back, you could see the unhappiness in their faces.

When we bought our house in Lincoln, having moved down from Scotland, the plan was to take both kids out of boarding school. By then, they had gone in very different directions. At school, Daniel was taunted by kids telling him his brother was odd. That began to push them apart. He wanted his brother to be there for him, but Ben was having enough trouble without trying to stick up for Daniel. And because Daniel was sporty, while Ben sang in the choir, their places within the school were very different. Daniel wasn't particularly happy when he found out he was leaving, but he did as he was told. We gave Ben the choice: Do A-levels where he was, or go to a school in Lincoln. And Ben said: 'They're going to make me a prefect, I'm captain at swimming, I'm going to stay.' So we thought things were OK. Ben was so honest and open, but he was also a good liar – he had to be.

CHAPTER 2

My Normal

Slapping and slopping down a coastal path on the Gower Peninsula, straight into the howl of Storm Abigail, I have never seen weather like it! Rain coming in off the Bristol Channel, horizontal. This doesn't sound like the best place to be, but I wouldn't want to be anywhere else. So many people told me I was crazy: 'How could you sell your house and everything you owned without knowing what the next step is?' But I found something that made me happy to my soul. And this is exactly it. Waves crashing against the cliffs, wind landing with its best shots. Fear. Mum's right, I was a good liar – I had a lot of practice. But I'm not lying anymore.

I haven't really thought this through. I've got no waterproof gear, so I'm soaked to the bone. I had a plan, but I kind of didn't. It's sink or swim, either you give up or you thrash away and get through it. It's just the two of us, me and a guy called Matt, from a running club near Swansea. I don't know what he's thinking, as we slap and slop away. Up on the cliff top I come to a halt. Abigail is howling straight at me as I look out to sea, and I'm howling back, arms outstretched:

'Come on! Come on, Abigail! Throw everything you fucking can at me! Come on, everything you've fucking got! I can take it! I can take anything!'

It's like something from a film, I half expect to be struck by a bolt of lightning. Meanwhile, Matt is keeping his distance, looking at me as if to say: 'What the hell have we got here?' He must think I've lost it. Completely lost it. I'm freezing, I'm drowning, I'm terrified. But I've never felt so alive.

. . . .

There were loads of kids being bullied at secondary school. And when other kids were being bullied it provided respite and relief for me. I'm ashamed to say there were even a couple of instances when I joined in. Once, I caught two kids in the act, so to speak, and ran up and down the corridor telling everybody about it, literally screaming at the top of my voice. It must have been hell for those kids, but I just thought: 'Well, at least I won't be bullied for a while.' You do what you have to do to survive in that kind of environment, it's dog eat dog, Darwinian. When you're the one taking the heat most of the time, if somebody else is being bullied for an afternoon, you'll gladly take the solace.

Even now, I think I played a big part in how my life unravelled. I can't just blame the bullies. Maybe if I'd been a little bit stronger, the bullying might have stopped. But I was in a constant battle with my inner self, that's how unhinged I was. Sometimes, I would find some strength from somewhere, put the shutters up and be able to block things out. I'd become older and more mature, which enabled me to put the face on and go into survival mode. The next day, I'd crash and be sobbing down the phone to Mum again. It was a life of desperation. I took GCSE music, but had no interest in music. I cheated in my exam, got one of the other kids to write one of my compositions for me. I was in the choir, but so were two of my bullies. They were everywhere I went, I couldn't escape them. I was terrible at most sport, a lanky streak of piss. I hated running, so cross-country in the freezing cold and mud, wearing a T-shirt and shorts and plimsolls, was hell to me.

My maths teacher was a kind soul. He was a dad, had two sons, and I found enjoyment in his subject. Sometimes he'd stand in for my housemaster and I'd really look forward to him being there because he made me feel safe. We'd have long chats and with his help, I got an A in one of my maths modules. I was over the moon, I'd never had an A in my life.

My other escape was swimming, which was the only sport I was mildly good at. My grandma was a champion swimmer, so I took after her, just as I took after her at picking flowers. I was good at swimming, fast. The weird part was that two of my bullies were on the team and in my final year, I was their captain. Being captain of the swimming team was easily my biggest achievement at school. It gave me a real sense of accomplishment, far more so than being a prefect. I suspect they only made me a prefect because not enough pupils wanted the gig. And you don't have to be a psychologist to see why swimming provided an escape – body submerged, goggles on, ears blocked, away from it all.

But swimming only provided temporary respite. That final year at school, the pressure was mounting and the lid was starting to rattle on the pot. I didn't like the way I looked, and I remember doing my hair in the mirror and nearly ripping it out because I couldn't get it perfect. I was hyper-stressed, frayed, stretched, frustrated and annoyed because I had no control over anything. But at the time, I didn't even recognise it as stress because it just became my normal. I could feel myself losing it, but because I had normalised the daily torture I couldn't see why I was losing it, which worried me even more. If somebody says something horrible to you, you obviously feel hurt; it gets to you, no matter how much you try to cover it up and say it hasn't. But because the bullying was such a constant in my life, people attacking me for who and what I was every single hour of every single day, with the occasional physical abuse thrown in for good measure, I became numb to the pain. In a sick way, I looked forward to it happening because it had become my normal. And if it didn't happen, I'd think: 'Oh my God, if not that, what else?' My perceptions had been reversed. I was losing a bit of my soul every single day, starting to question who I was, what I was, why was I different, why I was even here. Other people had hijacked my life, taken me over, and without even knowing it, I'd become a shell. It wasn't my life, it was a life for other people to mess with.

I don't remember there being a trigger and I didn't even hatch a plan to end things. One day, I just found myself putting that knife in my pocket, taking it back to my bedroom and cutting at my wrists. You can only bury all that poison for so long, eventually the body reacts. Looking back, it was one of the most important times in my life. I was so worried about the fact I'd tried to kill myself that I eventually told Mum and Dad when I got home. It was a massive shock to them.

* * * * * * * * * *

Beverley Smith, Ben's mum: *He got through the first part of his A-levels and was learning to drive when he came home to Lincoln at weekends. But he was getting thinner and thinner. He looked dreadful, yellow, haunted. Michaela, his German pal, who we thought was his girlfriend, rang me and said: 'Talk to Ben, please talk to Ben.' So one weekend, we had our quiet time together, and I said to him:*

'Something's going on, something's obviously going on.'

'No, I'm alright, Mum.'

'Don't you feel well?'

'Everything's fine…'

He was all packed up and ready to go back to school on Sunday evening, but we couldn't find him. I thought he was already in the car, but Pete came in and said: 'Where is he?' We searched the house, high and low, but couldn't find him. Eventually we found him in the garage, cowering in the corner, rocking backwards and forwards. He was in a terrible state. I brought him into the kitchen and said:

'Whatever is it? Whatever's the matter?'

'I tried to kill myself. With a knife. In my bedroom at school.'

'Why?!'

'I can't tell you, Mum, I can't tell you…'

I told him not to worry about going back to school, that he was never going back, that whatever it was, he was safe with us. And all he kept saying was: 'Don't be angry, please don't be angry.' I told him we weren't angry, that we were hurt and frightened for him, that we loved him very much and that he must have been desperate. He told us we didn't know the half of it, but still wouldn't give us any details. And when I asked what we could do to make it better, he took me by the hand, led me to the medicine cupboard in the kitchen and said: 'If you love me, you'll help me take all of these.' That's something no parent wants to see or hear. He was just so broken, so broken…

· · · · · · · · · ·

I can't remember any of that episode, Mum only told me about it a couple of years ago. That must have been the point at which I lost all semblance of control. Mum and Dad must have been terrified. That's when the decision was made to take me out of school. The one thing that hurt me about that was not being in the swimming team photo. My only real achievement, and there was no record of it.

After that, I had a complete nervous breakdown. That's a very sketchy period of my life, partly because I've suppressed it. Mum packed me off to see a counsellor, but I only went because I was told to. I wasn't really open to it, but I pretended to be: 'Yes, of course I'll talk about my feelings and everything else, deal with it all and everything will be OK…' As Mum says, I was a good liar. I didn't give that counsellor anything, but I must have done a pretty good job at seeming normal because I soon got a clean bill of health. Mum and Dad got me a private tutor and I somehow ended up with a C and an E in my maths and physics A-levels. So much for my education not suffering. But I don't want my parents to feel guilty; they went through so much shit as well. I know they never wanted to send us both to boarding school – I honestly believe they would have investigated all other options before making that choice – but sometimes life makes choices difficult.

. . . .

Marathon number 75 in the bag, I squelch my way back to the car park in Swansea, where Florence – my campervan – is resting. And what do you know? There's a parking ticket slapped on the windscreen. But it's going to take more than that to ruin my day. When you've been through what I went through – the beatings, the mental torture, the humiliation, the hollowing-out of the soul – what's a parking ticket? That night, I remember what Mum said to me, after finding out I tried to take my own life: 'There's a reason why you're here on this planet. You might not know what that reason is yet, but you will figure it out one day.'

A wise woman.

CHAPTER 3

A Little Bit Unhinged

B ut I'm getting ahead of myself. You're probably reading this book because you heard about this Challenge I cooked up and wondered what would make anybody want to do something so crazy. I've already touched upon my motivations, and those motivations will become much clearer. But first, let me tell you a bit about The 401 Challenge itself: a bit about how I came up with the idea and why I did it, but also about the planning, logistics and those all-important nuts and bolts that held the whole mad project together. Once you've got the picture, you can be with me every step of the way...

I'd always seen myself doing something big. Not necessarily completing 401 marathons in 401 days big, but something where I could say afterwards: 'That was different.' A lot of people do crazy challenges because they've had a lot of crap in their life, because there's nothing like going through crap in your life to make you realise that life is a finite thing. But I never viewed it as a case of trying to fix my soul or anything deep like that. I had dealt with a lot of the stuff from my past before I started planning The 401 Challenge and having dealt with it, this energy was released inside me. The time I used to spend worrying about stuff needed to be filled with something positive. I needed a new focus, a new direction; I needed an adventure. The 401 Challenge was it.

. . . .

Andy Davis, Ben's personal trainer: *When Ben first came to me, he was still smoking and very unfit. To be honest, he was a wreck. He had no muscle on him, 30 per cent body fat and you wouldn't have thought he was capable of running one marathon, let alone 401. He started getting fitter and losing weight, and one day he came into the gym and said: 'Andy, I've got something to tell you – I'm thinking about running 401 marathons in 401 days.' It was such a ridiculous task and I was worried for him. I told him he was mad, that his body would shut down after about 60. But he told me all about the bullying and just seemed so determined. I didn't try to talk him out of it, because I knew I wouldn't be able to. And from the moment he told me, I just knew he would finish. So I said: 'OK. This is the plan...'*

A few weeks in, he said to me: 'I've handed in my notice, so I'm really gonna have to do this Challenge now.' For eight months, Ben worked with me for three days a week and did weight training the rest of the time. By the time he started the Challenge, we'd got his body fat down to 14 per cent, he had quite a bit of muscle on him and he was as fit and ready as he was ever going to be.

• • • • • • • • • •

I also passionately believed that people shouldn't have to go through what I went through, so I knew I wanted to raise awareness and money for charities I really cared about. Kidscape and Stonewall do a lot of great work trying to prevent bullying in schools, but I still felt passionately that a lot of bullying in the UK was being swept under the carpet. You'd hear about it once a year, during Anti-Bullying Week, when it would be all over the TV and newspapers, and then there would be silence, other than when some poor family lost their son or daughter through bullying. So I wanted to spend a whole year, or more, raising the issue all over the UK. You don't want to be the only person shouting, you want lots of others to join in. I also wanted to challenge people, to inspire them to do different things, take what I got from running and give that to other people. But because I wasn't a celebrity, with the backing of the media and lots of financial help, I knew my Challenge had to be verging on the insane if I was going to raise anywhere near £250,000 for Kidscape and Stonewall, which I made my target.

• • • • • • • • • •

Nikki Kerr, head of fundraising at Kidscape: In May 2015, I got a call from Ben, completely out of the blue. He told me that he was attempting this challenge and wanted to raise money for Kidscape. I put down the phone, turned to my chief executive and said: 'I've just been speaking to someone who's going to run 401 marathons in 401 days.' She said: 'You what?' I'd had various people contact me with all sorts of hair-brained ideas, so I took Ben's with a pinch of salt. But he followed up with an email and more calls and it soon became apparent that he had thought about all the angles and was very serious about doing it. So I thought: 'Yeah, let's give this a go. What do we have to lose? If he 'only' manages to do 100 marathons, that's still an incredible achievement and would display the values of resilience that Kidscape shares.

He was so honest and open about why he was doing it, right from the start. I've had meetings with many, many people who have come up with a proposal but have hidden agendas or are not telling the whole story. But when Ben was telling me

*about his own experiences and why he wanted to do what
he was doing, I could tell it came straight from the heart. He
wasn't looking for personal gain, he did not want accolades
or celebrity status, he just really wanted to do what he could to
promote the work that we do.*

*For a small charity like us, it's vital to have advocates like
Ben, because we don't have a big marketing budget. The
more people talk about bullying, the more likely other people
are going to say: 'This is happening to me or somebody I
know.' And Kidscape can help. The consequences of not
talking about bullying are many. You might not achieve as well
academically as you might have done; you might find it very
hard to have relationships because you don't trust people; it
can affect your work life. It affects people until their dying day.
People in their 80s and 90s can still remember in great detail
things that happened to them when they were eight years
old, even the names of their bullies. Kidscape's vision is for all
children to grow up in a world free from bullying.*

· · · · · · · · · ·

When I initially came up with the idea – more about that later – I
wanted it to be fluid, allowing room for the project to grow organically.
But because I'd been working in the corporate world and had done
quite a lot of project management work, I figured that if I wanted it to
succeed, I had to have a solid structure in place. To fund the project,
I initially used the money from the sale of my house, along with any
belongings I felt I didn't need. Drastic, I know, but corporate sponsors
didn't exactly clamber on board. And after clearing debts, visiting
different countries to train and buying various other bits and pieces,

I was left with about £4,000. I had to pay for accommodation, petrol, food and various sundries – for 401 days – so we knew we'd have to rely on operational donations from individuals and sell a lot of 401 merchandise.

Mum and Dad kindly bought me a campervan, which I would eat in, wash in, work in and, hopefully only occasionally, sleep in – and as no one else was in a position to come with me, I would be in the van on my own. I would also drive it to the start of my route every morning, and to wherever I needed to be after that day's marathon was run. I named the campervan Florence, after my Grandma, who passed away a few years earlier. Grandma was very loving and one of those people you knew you could always rely on. She was also very strong-willed, driven and independent. Had she still been with us, Grandma probably would have dropped everything and come with me.

Having drawn up a detailed route with Dad, outlining exactly where I would be on any given day, we contacted running clubs all over the country, asking them to help organise a marathon course for when I was passing through, as well as keep me company on the way round. Let's face it, running 401 marathons in 401 days on your own could send a man quite mad, and those people I hoped to run with would be key to keeping me sane and spreading the message further afield. Because I didn't want to spend too many nights in the van, or pay for too many hotel rooms, we also hoped running club members would be kind enough to put me up for the night, feed me, let me use their shower and do my laundry. Physiotherapy would obviously be of paramount importance, so the plan was to contact therapists and ask if they'd mind giving me a post-marathon rub-down for free. The 401 Challenge was clearly going to rely heavily on the kindness of strangers – and my wonderful, crack 401 team.

Because the whole operation was run on a shoestring, every member of the 401 team was an unpaid volunteer. Dad was appointed head of logistics; Mum would look after accommodation, physio, and finances; Tolu Osinnowo was brought in as project manager, also in charge of branding; Vicky Burr would look after the media side of things; I'd look after the social media, often from the back of the van; and Kyle would kind of oversee everything. But much more of Kyle later…

· · · · · · · · · · ·

Tolu Osinnowo, 401 project manager: *I heard of Ben's challenge through social media. I was so intrigued so I got in touch, and we just clicked. We were on the phone for ages, talking about why bullying was so close to his heart. But I was on the dole, really needed to get a paid job to pay my bills, and generally wasn't coping very well. I thought I was worthless, was really depressed, having anxiety attacks. I was actually a little bit suicidal. But I didn't tell Ben about any of this, I hid it.*

Ben phoned me two or three months later and said: 'Hi Tolu, I've found two new charities that might be able to support me with this – Kidscape and Stonewall – and I'd really like you to be my project manager. You had some really good ideas and I think you just get what I'm trying to do.' I was part-time managing a bar, but I thought I'd be able to manage 10 hours a week, and it just snowballed from there. Initially, the plan was pretty much Ben just running a marathon every day for 401 days, but then all these other things started coming into play: how were we going to get money to support Ben? How were we going to pay for food? How were we going to promote it? It quickly turned into this really big machine, and we realised it needed to be a brand, with merchandising to go with it. I studied graphic design at uni, so I'd come up with all these ideas, send them over, and his reaction was always: 'Oh my God, Tolu! This is amazing, exactly what I had in mind.' We never really talked things through, but it always seemed to work. It was really weird how in sync we were.

. . . .

BEN'S 401 CONSECUTIVE MARATHONS TO COMBAT BULLYING

BRISTOL EVENING POST, 1 SEPTEMBER 2015

'...Between now and October 5, 2016 Ben, 33, plans to run a remarkable 10,506 miles – the equivalent of here to Sydney, Australia. To do so he will have to take on board 2.4 million calories – around 6,000 a day – and spend around 2,400 hours running...'

. . . .

DAY 1: It's 1 September 2015, the morning of the first of what I hope will be 401 marathons, and all I can think is: 'Shit, I'm not ready for this.' We'd anticipated there wouldn't be a massive send-off, and when I turned up to Bristol's Millennium Square that morning, there were six of us, including a few friends from work, my local running club and my friend's dog. A couple of people in suits wander past, eye up my van, parked in the middle of the square – you can't miss it for The 401 Challenge branding – and I can see them thinking: 'What the bloody hell is that all about?'

That was the general reaction: 'You're doing what? Running 401 marathons? In a row? Are you serious? No chance! I wouldn't even bother.' People looked at me as if I'd lost my mind. Some people didn't think I'd start The 401 Challenge, let alone finish it. I found it a little bit frustrating to start with, but I came to expect it. And then I learned to ignore it. I'd walk away thinking: 'OK, that's your opinion, but I'm going to prove you wrong.'

Maybe you do have to be a little bit unhinged to even consider running 401 marathons in a row, but who says I'm the mad one? Maybe it's the rest of you. There's a madness about complaining and whingeing and not doing anything about it, especially when you know you've only got one life. And those people who complain and whinge about their own lives are the first to judge anybody trying to live their life differently. That had been me, constantly telling myself I needed to change my circumstances, but I did bugger all about it for so long. I only had myself to blame; I was so hell-bent on achieving everything I'd been told I had to achieve to be successful in life, from when I was a kid, and I was scared of the alternatives, terrified to even consider thinking in a different way. I'd settled, told myself: 'No, I'm fine with my lot. If anybody else wants to do something different, I'll watch from a distance.' How awful is that? One life, and I'd settled on how it was going to roll out, from my 20s until the day I was old and grey. That's where I was. And I wasn't happy. But I stepped back from the situation and thought: 'I don't want to live this life anymore. I don't know what life I want to live, but I know it's not this one. But if this isn't happiness, what is? Maybe if I start to think in a different way, I'll find it. What if I get rid of the money and the possessions? That makes sense, because I can categorically say they're not making me happy. And once they're gone, maybe I'll have a clearer idea of what happiness is.' I suddenly realised you can do what you want, when you want to do it. If you really want to.

· · · · · · · · · ·

I opened the medicine cabinet, unscrewed all the bottles I could see, scattered pills all over the kitchen floor and thought: 'I've tried this before, so it would be easy enough to try it again. Only this time it might just work.' Sitting there, I just felt so sad, so heartbroken and so alone. Call it complacency, call it a subconscious desire to be caught, call it whatever you want, but my wife had discovered my secret. I hadn't been cheating, but I had begun to explore my sexuality, looking at men having sex on the computer. I was usually very careful to clear the history, like you do. This one time, I'd forgotten. It's amazing how such small things can have such huge ramifications.

We'd only been married for two months and I was visiting one of my accounts in the North. Driving back down the motorway from York to Bristol, I was shattered – I couldn't wait to get home and slump in front of the TV. But when I walked through the front door, she was waiting for me. She gave me a hug as if everything was normal, before we went into the lounge. But everything was far from normal. After revealing she'd discovered my secret, I became desperate, like a beggar on his knees, trying to gather up the scattered scraps of his life. I must have made for a pathetic sight, but I felt so very guilty and regretful.

After my excuses had dried up, she walked out and went straight to her brother's house, while I slumped to the floor, still wearing my suit, thinking: 'That's it. It's over.' I was terrified of being left alone, just like that young boy walking the dark corridors at school, feeling for the walls, not knowing what I might find and what they might throw at me the following morning. That's when I opened the pills and thought: 'It would be easier for everybody if I took these and disappeared.' But just like when I was that young boy, sitting on my bed and cutting at my wrists with a knife, I couldn't finish the job.

After I put the pills back in their bottles, finally peeled myself off the floor and climbed the stairs, I could see myself, as if I was having an outer-body experience. In bed, I stared up at the ceiling, every tick of the alarm clock like a dull peck to my temple. When I went downstairs the following morning, I was still consumed by fear. Then, suddenly, I heard a key in the door and in she walked. Instead of being angry, her brother had said: 'Men do stupid things. Just give him another chance, listen to him.' So she gave me a big hug and said: 'Let's give this a go, let's work through this.' She didn't ask me if I was gay, but I told her I didn't know who I was. I was just so grateful that she had forgiven me and come back. I kicked everything that had happened the previous evening into the long grass. From my whole life falling out from underneath me, suddenly everything was fixed. Except, of course, it wasn't. Actually, the lid had been ripped right off, I just couldn't see it yet.

• • • • • • • • • •

I got married in August 2013, when I was 31, and our wedding day was a really happy occasion. It was nerve-wracking, but I wouldn't go as far as to say it didn't feel right. I certainly wasn't walking to the altar thinking: 'I shouldn't be doing this.' It was a day I'd accepted had to happen, so it might as well be a happy one. Because I was leading this fake life, I thought getting married was the right thing to do. I'd become comfortable and, dare I say it, happy. Or at least I'd tricked myself into thinking I was happy with it. She was my companion, my best friend and I loved her. I found my wife extremely attractive. Most people think that if you're a gay man you can only fancy men, and if you're a straight man you can only fancy women. I don't necessarily think that's true. In my opinion, you can fall in love with the person, regardless of their sex. That's what happened with me.

I wasn't the only one kidding myself I was in a healthy relationship, and the illusion of a functioning marriage could only last so long. We hobbled on through Christmas, putting on a face, although I didn't do a very good job. That Christmas was hell. I felt like I didn't have any control. The lid had been lifted and, try as I might, I couldn't shut it. My insides were starting to seep over the top and I was reacting to things in ways I wouldn't normally. We tried to talk but I would be verbally aggressive, start crying or shut down completely and show no emotion. In the end, she suggested I see a counsellor, so I did. This time I was 100 per cent honest and the counsellor started to help me accept who I was. It was scary, because I didn't know whether I was ready to hear that.

. . . .

Beverley Smith, Ben's mum: *As long as Ben is happy, we're happy, no matter what he decides to do. On his wedding day, I was pinning the flower on his jacket and I said to him: 'You are sure, aren't you? Because if we're going to do a runner, we'll have to do it now.' It was only a joke, but I'd been married and divorced before I met Pete, and I wish somebody had suggested that on my first wedding day! Ben replied: 'We have talked about this and this is what we want.' Little did we know what was going on in Ben's head.*

He started to put on weight and was always stressed. He'd explain it away by saying work was getting on top of him, which made sense, because he was working for a big corporate company. Ben is a perfectionist and he'd spend hour upon hour getting his work right, sometimes until 5 o'clock in the morning. There was love between Ben and his wife, the two of them got on very well. But they didn't visit that often because they were always too busy, and never seemed to be around when we suggested going to visit them. Then, out of the blue, a couple of months after he got married, he sent us a letter, telling us we didn't understand him and he didn't want us in his life anymore. He didn't even say: 'I'm thinking things through, I'll contact you.' I said to Pete: 'We've lost him.'

We thought he might have been to therapy, the counsellor had told him to put his thoughts down on paper and he'd posted it, instead of filing it away. But I still don't know for sure why he wrote that letter. I think he was going into crisis. Maybe he thought, if he cut us free, we wouldn't be hurt by what was to come. Maybe he was trying to protect us again. Whatever the reasons, it broke our hearts. I was told for a long time that

I could never have kids, so to have Ben and Daniel was such a gift. At times, we didn't get things right, because no parent does. Children don't come with a book of instructions, so all you can do is your very best by them. And all we'd ever done for both our children was motivated by love.

. . . .

I just wanted simplicity in my life, which is how I started to drift apart from my parents. Because I was battling so much inside, it seemed easier to remove Mum and Dad from the equation. It wasn't a case of wanting to protect them from anything, I was just stuck between a rock and a hard place. I made the wrong choice, and that's how the letter came about.

I worked my way through to the beginning of February, when I moved out of the house and into the local Premier Inn, to give my wife time to think. I was meant to be gone for a week, but after three days she said she'd done her thinking and wanted to meet. I was sitting on the bed in my hotel room when she told me it was over. I couldn't believe it, I was in complete dismay. My life was like a Jenga puzzle, with my wife at the bottom, propping the whole thing up. I thought it would all come crashing down if you removed her. We'd been together for almost 10 years, so our lives were so intertwined.

I just wanted this life of a 'normal' person, but it went too far, and I'm sorry for that. I didn't mean to hurt her, but now I was fearful this plan I'd had in my head since I was a teenager was falling to pieces. I was worried what people would think of me when they found out. The idea of anyone thinking bad of me filled me with dread. I thought it would end me. The day she told me she wanted to end it was the worst day of my life. But probably the best, too.

. . . .

Millennium Square begins filling up as start time approaches and a small crowd of family and friends begins to gather. It's a beautiful day, warm and sunny. The press has turned up – the *Bristol Post*, local TV – as well as a sprinkling of old workmates, running club friends and family. Mum is selling wristbands out of the front of the van and there's a real market stall mentality about the whole thing. It feels small, but like something that will grow organically. At least some people have bought into it, although I'm not sure how many of them have complete faith. It ticks round to 10 o'clock and off I go, wondering what's going to happen, where this journey is going to take me, whether I'm going to be OK, and whether I've made a mistake.

Maybe they're right not to have faith. Halfway round that first marathon, I'm thinking: 'Oh shit, what the bloody hell have I done?' My running buddy Susan has planned the course and she hasn't given me a flat one as a gentle introduction. In fact, it's bloody hilly, and I'm cursing her all the way round: 'How could she do this to me?' I wanted to kill her. But it's spectacular at the same time, running with good friends, including Vicky Burr, who props me up for the last couple of miles. Day one complete and I've survived! Afterwards, I pick up the van, drive to Gordano Services and head to Starbucks. And while I'm sitting there, nursing a flat white, I'm thinking: 'What will happen along the way?' I've got 400 more days of unknown stretched out ahead of me. I rolled the dice, created a life for me. And the really exciting part is, I don't really know what it is yet.

CHAPTER 4

Rationalising Madness

Day two in Bristol is the same route as day one, although this time I cover the full 26.2 miles with a great guy called Andy, who owns a coffee shop in Bristol and is training for his Land's End to John o' Groats run. Andy has turned up at exactly the right time because he gets what I'm trying to achieve completely, rather than looking at me as if I'm absolutely nuts. You need people like Andy because they make the apparently absolutely nuts seem almost normal.

DAYS 2–7: When I leave Bristol at the end of day two, and realise I'm not going to be back for 50-odd days, it feels like I've strayed too far from the shore. It's not as if I feel stranded, but a reality hits me: 'There's no going back now, too much of me has been invested. I have no choice but to plough on…' More hills in Portishead, which is where I call home, but the views from the coastal path, of Cardiff, Newport and the Severn Bridge, keep things sweet. Tim from the local running club has planned the course, which takes us past some fishing boats, parked in the middle of a forest, apparently part of some art exhibition. It's a surreal sight, and slightly unsettling, because I suddenly wonder if those boats might be me soon, lost and forgotten, marooned where I don't belong.

Travelling downhill – trail running was never my strong point – I go over on my knee. It hurts, but I keep on going, and I don't realise I've damaged it as badly as I have. Over the next four days, it gets progressively worse. By day seven, it's doubled in size. Tim feels guilty: 'Great, I've already killed him.' That's already a running joke, members of running clubs saying to me: 'We don't want to be the ones who damaged or broke you…' On top of the gammy knee, I've also got tendinitis in my left shin and a suspected fracture in one of my toes. It doesn't sound ideal, and it's only day three, but I tell myself I have to go through that at the beginning. It forces my body to ask the question: 'What the hell are you doing to me? It's not right!' But as time goes on, my body starts saying: 'Alright, you're not going to listen to me, so I might as well fall into line.' And the fact the problem started in my knee and moved downwards into my toes suggests it is exiting my body. That's what I've decided to tell myself anyway. Well, you've got to stay positive…

I work my way down through Somerset and into Devon, taking in part of a 24-hour race in Taunton, the Long Run in the Meadow. This is my first proper night in Florence and I'm not prepared. I buy some chicken from the local supermarket and spend about an hour trying to cook it in the oven. I realise I haven't filled the van with water, so I can't shower, and end up eating my chicken thighs on the bed and falling asleep stinking.

On day six, the Forever Running Club from Taunton are out in force to support me, and we follow a route shaped like a flower petal, flitting between the town, the canal and the glorious Quantock Hills. In Exeter, I stay with the guys from the local fire station and they treat me to a roast dinner, and I'm able to fill Florence with water and charge her up. Day seven, and I'm on my own for the first time. The guy who planned the route greets me at the start but is working, and nobody from the local running club has made it. I don't blame them, people have commitments. My family friends, Ian and Rosie, surprise me, having come all the way over from Germany, and it's lovely to see them. But it's 30°C, I'm lonely, my legs are in bits and I'm only partially comfortable running uphill. All the aches and pains are starting to play on my mind and zap my motivation. So much for the positivity. I'd been on such a high, and now I've come crashing down to earth. I start out jogging, then start walking, and end up shuffling. My phone won't get a signal, I get lost, run out of water and end up covering 29 miles in about eight hours. My confidence is through the floor and I'm thinking: 'There might be a lot more of these...' I'm already sick of it and I've still got 394 marathons to go.

I park in an industrial estate just outside Exeter, head to a supermarket and stock up on water and frozen peas, to reduce the swelling on my knee. When I come back, Florence isn't there. In a panic, I start scanning the car park, hoping I'm just so tired that I've forgotten where I put her, but also terrified she's been stolen. Everything I have is in Florence – is this the end of the Challenge? Two guys approach me and one of them pulls out his phone. On the screen, it reads: 'Your van is in a tree'. He's used Google to translate it from Lithuanian to English. Florence isn't actually in a tree, but she has rolled into one because I forgot to put the handbrake on.

I just want to go home.

. . . .

The moment my wife said, 'It's over', it set the wheels in motion. In a cowardly way, I was relieved she'd made the decision because I wasn't strong enough to. The split was amicable, and clean. I moved into a flat on the marina in Portishead and we put the house on the market and split the difference. I sold my shares in the company I worked for, bought loads of furniture for the new flat and started the long journey of trying to figure out me.

I truly believe that I had to go through everything I did to be the person I am now. As such, I stand by my choices. But I honestly think that if I hadn't had running, I wouldn't have got through my divorce. Just after we separated, I was due to run the Barcelona Marathon, the first of 18 I had scheduled for 2014. My wife was supposed to be coming with me and was on every ticket, so I didn't want to go to Spain. But my brother Dan dropped everything, drove down and persuaded me to go. He even came with me, and I'm so glad he did. He also told me to contact Mum and Dad, which I did. Mum told me how much my letter, which I'd sent only a couple of months earlier, had hurt her, which was understandable. But I didn't really explain anything. Because I was still so submissive and meek, I just took it. But running was already making me stronger. In fact, it was the one thing that gave me the strength to do everything I've done since. It would be too dramatic to say running saved my life, but it allowed me to work out what my life was going to be.

When I was 29, I had something called a Transient Ischaemic Attack (TIA), or a 'mini-stroke'. I was sitting at my desk at work and my sight went, as if somebody had drawn a black curtain across my face. On top of that, I temporarily lost the feeling in my left arm and developed tinnitus in my left ear. My colleague read out all the symptoms on the NHS website and it said: 'Go to hospital'. It might sound terrifying, but I was just so dead inside that I didn't really feel much about anything. It was more a case of: 'Oh, OK, this is happening now...' I thought the nurse at the hospital was going to tell me I was stressed, so when she explained what had actually happened to me, it was a bit of a shock. But maybe it shouldn't have been. I had so much internal turmoil because of hiding who I really was; I was 16 and a half stone; smoking a pack a day, maybe more; drinking too much. I had a high-pressure job as an operations executive that I'd become totally immersed in, because, albeit on a subconscious level, it meant I didn't have to confront who I truly was. Like so many people, I'd just drifted into this existence. And that's all I was really doing – existing. When the TIA happened, the doctor told me to start looking after myself and I knew something had to change. It was an epiphany, but not like in the movies. Things didn't suddenly become great, they actually grew worse before they got better. I'd conditioned myself over so many years to think in a certain way, so to suddenly change overnight was not going to be possible.

On the list of 500 things I wanted to do in my life, running was about 500th. I was that classic guy who bought a gym membership in January and cancelled it a month later. I'd been out for a few jogs but never found a passion for it. When a work colleague dragged me down to Southville Running Club in Bedminster, Bristol, I felt like my 10-year-old self again. I was putting myself in a situation I didn't really want to be in, this time where everyone was skinny and fit and I was going to come in last. I was terrified. I wasn't a runner, I couldn't run for a bus. To this day, I don't really know why I went. I ran and walked a couple of miles, but I wasn't the only one walking, so I didn't feel like a failure. People didn't point at me and laugh. I went home that night with this feeling of accomplishment, thinking: 'You know what? I quite enjoyed that.' So I went back the next week. And I kept on going, week after week, paying my 50p to run on a Tuesday night.

Within six months, I'd done my first 5k, 10k and half-marathon, and in 2013 I did my first marathon in Brighton. I ran the first 19 miles and everything was going to plan, before I stopped for a wee and seized up. The last seven miles were hell. Running along the seafront towards the pier, I could see the finish line in the distance, but my body hurt and I was exhausted. But I was utterly focused on finishing. After I crossed the line, I collapsed on the floor, someone put a medal around my neck and I cried. I'd finished in a respectable four and a half hours, and I was hooked.

Two days later, I booked up for the Amsterdam Marathon, because I wanted to do better. Running was making me fit and healthy, I was feeling better about myself, more confident, because I was running further and it was getting easier. It was incredibly invigorating just doing something I'd never done before – 'There is an alternative!' I liked the fact I was achieving things I never thought I could, conquering new ground. And I loved the sociability and companionship of the running club, making new friends, with like-minded people – my own friends, not people I was expected to be friends with. Running created this wonderful new world for me. And it felt like I was figuring out my own place in it, at last.

I used to call running my filing time. I'd have a horrible day at work, come home full of stress, my brain addled, put my trainers on and disappear for an hour. To begin with I ran with music, maybe to take my mind off the pain, but I soon stopped doing that because I liked to take in everything around me – the scenery, the conversations, the laughter. By the time I got back from a run, it felt like everything in my mind had been tidied up and filed away. For the first time in my life, I felt organised. And running rekindled my love of travel and adventure, which I'd had as a child, and made me feel free. So, when I split from my wife, running had equipped me to deal with the inevitable fallout.

· · · · · · · · · ·

24-HOUR RUN IN TAUNTON? EASY WHEN YOU'RE DOING 401 MARATHONS IN 401 DAYS

SOMERSET COUNTY GAZETTE, 8 SEPTEMBER 2015

'...Ben has already raised £3,500 of his target of £250,000, to be split between anti-bullying charities Kidscape and Stonewall...'

· · · · · · · · · ·

DAYS 8–9: When I wake up, my knee is bigger than ever and I don't know if I'll be able to run at all. But about eight miles in, my legs start working. One of the lads from the local fire station keeps me company, and the views along the coast from Dawlish to Exeter are stunning. Suddenly, everything is good again. I pass 200 miles since the start of the Challenge and celebrate on the quayside with a flat white and a bowl of nachos. By the end of day eight, I've set a new PB – eight marathons in eight days. Looking back, I'm glad I had that horrible day as early as I did, because I was able to use it as a tool and tell myself: 'It will never be as bad as that.' When we were planning The 401 Challenge, Mum often used to say to me: 'Look what you've faced, look what you've been through – if you can get through all of that, you can get through anything this Challenge throws at you.' All those horrible days I'd stored up were my preventative medicine.

Day nine, and the Newton Abbot Marathon is like having a full recharge. The Teignbridge Trotters are out in force and Richard (17 miles) and Suzie (13 miles) run further than they've ever done. I've also met a guy called Smokes, a sub three-hour marathon man who puffed his way through 10 cigarettes during the course of the run. You *really* shouldn't be able to do that. He told me he quit for a while and his times got worse, so he started again and his times improved. Today, things are really starting to take shape, with people plugging into the project, feeling inspired and doing things they've never done before. And it works both ways, because I'm inspired and energised by them. I've still got a swollen knee, but I've realised that if the mind isn't right, and there is doubt and negativity, it's like wading through treacle. You really do have the ability to change the way you are by changing the way you think.

* * * * * * * * *

Suzie Mills, Teignbridge Trotters: *When I first heard about Ben, I thought he had to be nuts for doing what he was doing. People were voicing all sorts of doubts: 'He's obviously going to get injured at some point. How's he going to cope with the winter weather? There's just no way he's going to do this.' I was intrigued nonetheless, so a couple of days before he was due to be passing through, I thought: 'You know what? I'd really like to join him.' A very understanding boss gave me the day off and I joined Ben at about mile six or seven. I was petrified, because I didn't want to slow Ben, and everybody else, down. But I needn't have worried, he was just so inclusive and supportive. And after speaking to him and finding out why he was doing what he was doing, how passionate he was, feeling his determination and seeing the support he was getting, I thought: 'You know what? If he can get this kind of support all the way round, he might just pull this off.'*

He did seem a little bit crazy, which you have to be to take on a challenge of that magnitude. But he was also very humble, and not afraid to be open and honest about why he was doing it – about his mental health issues, the bullying and the struggles with his sexuality. I think people responded to that openness and honesty. I know I did. I'm always quite guarded when I meet new people, but he was very disarming, and he got me to open up and be honest, with him and myself. He has a natural gift, without a doubt – it just seemed so easy to talk to him without fear of being judged. I think that's why the project ended up being so successful, and I think it was possibly a revelation to him that he had this special gift. After that first day, it already felt like we were really good friends. My plan was to do six or seven miles to show my support, but I ended up running 13. I was shocked, and it took a long time for it to sink in. A couple of weeks later, I ran with him again, from Feock to Portreath and back again, and he got me to open up a little bit more.

I suffered with depression, probably from when I was in my teens. I went to an all-girls school and spent my whole time there trying to work out where I fitted in. I wouldn't say I was bullied in the classic sense, I just never felt like I belonged. I wasn't sporty or academic or arty or musical, so I kind of drifted. I turned to food for comfort, so struggled with my weight, and that snowballed at university, where I still couldn't work out who I was. I didn't really do anything about my depression until I was in my 30s, when I arrived at a really bad place. It took me a long time to find out where I belonged, and it's not until the last six or seven years that I've really become happy in myself. Running definitely accelerated that process.

It was a drunken conversation with some friends, who were members of the Teignbridge Trotters, that led me to do my first run on 5 January 2015. Not that you could really call it running – I covered three miles in an hour. It was cold, dark and miserable. But I loved it. Growing up, I was the fat kid, picked last for everything, so I was worried about trailing behind at the back and holding everyone else up. But everyone was so supportive. It didn't matter that I was slow, others were happy to run at my pace, and I felt included in something for the first time in ages.

I took antidepressants, on and off, for about four years, and they kind of numb you. Taking tablets does stop the real lows, but it also stops you enjoying life, because you're just existing. Running allowed me to control my mental state. It has just brought everything together, made me a much happier person. I was well on my way before I met Ben, but he pushed me to really believe in myself, which I'd never really had before. To

*hear that from a stranger – 'Yeah, you can do it' – actually
meant more than close friends saying it. He didn't know me,
but he wanted me to succeed and do amazing things.*

*Ben was broken once, but managed to find the strength,
confidence and determination to go out and change his life.
More than that, he wanted to do something for other people.
That inspired me immensely. He showed people that it is
possible to be down and almost out before turning things
around. Because he was so open and honest about what he'd
been through, he gave people the strength to push and fight
and really find out who they were. He fed off seeing people
gain strength from him, so everyone was feeding off each
other. He was like some kind of eccentric travelling therapist,
doling out great dollops of hope wherever he went.*

· · · · · · · · · ·

DAY 10: Down through Torquay – where I almost get flattened by a
rogue wave – Paignton, Brixham and the breathtaking Berry Head,
where Torbay Athletics Club does its bit and Vicky Burr pops up again
to run the last two miles with me. I'm sure I'll see some incredible
scenery on my way round Britain, but it will have to go some way to
beat South Devon. I'm fed for free by the Riviera Centre, before going
back to Katie, Guy and their puppy Milo's house for some therapy.

Now the Facebook messages are starting to come in, which suggests
word is getting out and people are starting to understand what we're
trying to achieve. People are sharing my story, letting each other know
when I'm passing through their area, things are starting to grow, like
a tree, with roots going deeper and branches firing off in different
directions. More and more people are doing things they never thought
they could do, and celebrating it on social media. The project is

starting to get a reputation for being an inclusive thing, rather than a 'look at me' kind of thing. I'm already a bit sick of talking about myself, so that's a bit of a relief. Keeping up with all the social media – the daily posts, the video diary entries, the comments, the likes – is tough, because I'm doing it all myself. But there are others pulling the strings from behind the scenes…

• • • • • • • • • •

Pete Smith, Ben's dad: *I ran major operations rooms for the Royal Air Force, and my last major operational job was running combat air over Afghanistan. That's the world I'm from, dealing with problems, planning ahead. The joke was that I had a map of Britain laid out on the dining room table and was pushing Ben's van around the country with one of those long, croupier-style pushing sticks. But it's true, I became totally immersed in it – helping to organise the 401 was fun for me.*

    Ben hadn't even thought about doing risk assessments, and I'm not talking about those half-arsed risk assessments businesses make you do. What happens if you get injured and you can't run for a week, or a month, or ever again? How are you going to deal with it? Let's think about it now, so that we've got an answer if it happens. What happens if your van breaks down or weather prevents you from getting to your scheduled destination? Maybe you can just run around a track for two or three days, until we get the van back? You don't want to be dealing with those kinds of problems the second they occur because you'll be doing the hair-on-fire routine. Any plan must have lots of options built into it.

We looked at the weather two or three days ahead, the roads he was taking, the topography of his courses. I'd be on Google Earth working out if he could get his van to people's houses. Otherwise, people would say: 'Yeah, of course he can park his van outside.' And he'd turn up and the road would be too narrow. I'd look at all these things to make sure I could see any problems before they occurred, so that Ben didn't have to think and could just get on with his running. He'd ring up, tell me his problem and I'd say: 'Fine, you get on with what you're doing, I'll sort it and text you the solution.'

* * * * * * * * * *

When we were planning the Challenge, we'd approach potential corporate sponsors and say:

'This is what we're going to do – 401 marathons in 401 days.'
They'd usually say: 'What's your experience?'
'Well, I've done 30 marathons in two years, but I've never done any-thing like this before… Hello? Hello? Are you still there?'

Most of the time, that was the end of the conversation. I don't know if they just thought it was foolhardy, ridiculous or both, because I didn't get much feedback. But I understood it was a big risk for anyone to commit, because they had no idea if I'd be able to pull it off. Had I been them, I would have had grave doubts as well. I was 33 and had only been running for four years. It's not as if I was Sir Ranulph Fiennes, with a long track record of doing all these mad, amazing things. So, in the absence of paid staff, my unpaid 401 team of volunteers were manning the fort while I was out on the road. Vicky Burr came on board as media manager, after seeing a plea from Tolu on the website Pimp My Cause, which connects people in the charity sector. The team was scattered all over the country: Mum (accommodation, physio and finances) and Dad (logistics) were in Lincoln; Tolu (project manager and branding) was in Brighton; Vicky (media) was in Weybridge; and Kyle (pretty much everything) was in Bristol. And because none of us had any experience of planning anything like it, we were having to learn on the hoof.

• • • • • • • • • •

Tolu Osinnowo, 401 project manager: *I'd always told myself that there was something I was going to be a part of that would be huge and change a lot of people's lives. Within the first month, it dawned on me that The 401 Challenge was that thing. We came up with all sorts of crazy ideas in those early days. Milk Tray were recruiting for a new Milk Tray Man, and I thought: 'Oh my God, Ben would be an amazing Milk Tray Man – he could talk to kids in the morning, run a marathon in the afternoon and deliver chocolates in the evening.' But he never got shortlisted, much to his relief! Not everything came off, because the team was so small, but Ben always believed in my abilities. He used to say on the phone: 'You know what, Tolu? You are bloody amazing! I don't know how you do what you do.' The fact that Ben had trusted me with this massive project, where I could be as creative as possible, and believed in my abilities, meant so much to me.*

• • • • • • • • • •

We contacted about 200 running clubs before I set off, but some of them thought I'd never reach them. One of them said: 'I'm so sorry,

I didn't think you'd make it as far as us, so I haven't really organised anything.' That's what happens when you attempt something for the first time, you come up against a lot of natural cynicism, scepticism and wariness. We had every intention of contacting every media outlet in every area, but we didn't pull things together in time, so we started using running clubs to get the message out instead.

We were finding out what worked and what didn't as we went along, and we got so much wrong. I was going to have a GoPro strapped to my chest, but that lasted about 30 seconds, because, frankly, I didn't know how to work it and I couldn't be bothered trying to find out. So I chucked it in the van and it never came out again. The first marathon taught me to keep it simple, never over-complicate things, take it for what it is. The running itself simplified everything: 'I don't need this and that, I just need to go out and run 26.2 miles every day. It doesn't matter how long it takes, if I get lost, if I can't get Wi-Fi, if nobody turns up to support me, my job is to run and then move on'. It was about trying to rationalise madness, normalise things, view it as a job, but a job I wanted to do. But because I'd finally found what I wanted to do with my life and what made me happy, it gave me joy. So even though I viewed it as a job, it didn't feel like one.

. . . .

DAYS 11–16: In Dartmouth on day 11, my knee stands up to the hilliest course I've run so far, I'm gobsmacked by the sight of Slapton Sands, Dartmouth AAC share the view with me and the Little Cotton Caravan Park lets me stay the night for free. The generosity of people is beginning to overwhelm me. People keep telling me I'm an inspiration, which I don't know how to take.

On day 12, the Plymouth Harriers lead me up into Dartmoor, where I do two laps of a reservoir, and when I return to the van that night, I discover that Stephen Fry has tweeted his support. Because he's got about a billion followers, Twitter is going ballistic, my phone won't stop pinging and I can't sleep. But credit to him, he was one of our first celebrity endorsers and took our message far beyond these shores.

A wonderful chiropractor called Michelle manipulates my body back into place on day 13 and then it's on to Saltash for my first run in Cornwall, where Helen Roper of the Tamar Trotters – a nutcase just like me, but one of the nicest ones you'll meet – knocks out a cool 26.2 miles. On day 15, I run in Liskeard, which is a weird experience, because that's where I got married. But I decide it's nice to be back, secure and happy. In Pensilva, I am greeted by a handful of kids in running gear. They run the first half a mile with me, but as I approach the school gates, I can hear more kids roaring my name. They unfurl a banner, and although it makes me feel embarrassed, it's all so lovely at the same time.

Clive from the campsite dusts off his trainers and runs with me every step of the way. And all the time I'm running, wherever I am in the country, I'm hearing stories – heartbreaking stories, inspirational stories, stories people have never told anybody else before. When you're in a suit or an office or any structured environment, you're expected to think and behave in a certain way; there are barriers to being who you really are. But when you're running, those barriers just melt away. Take that person out of their suit or the office or any structured environment, put them on a coastal path in Cornwall, and he or she will open up to anybody. Without meaning to sound pretentious, running takes you to a higher level of consciousness, so that you are able to see the bigger picture, and it's also a democratising experience. So, a couple of weeks in, The 401 Challenge, as I'd hoped, is growing organically, with people mucking in and offering support, but also lapping up the energy, finding their voice, opening up and taking away from the experience whatever they need to.

CHAPTER 5

A Beautiful Mind

DAYS 17–27: More kindness at the Eden Project on day 17, where I'm given a free Snoozebox – which is basically a sleeping pod – for the night, and a deep sleep is essential because the following day's marathon is a complete and utter bastard, albeit in a wonderful way. On top of a tor, I get a view of the north and south coasts, up as far as Newquay and down as far as Fowey; and on the streets of Truro, locals stop and shout: 'You're that guy running all those marathons! How do I donate?' It's beautiful words like that that keep me going. On a country lane, I come face-to-face with a herd of cows. One cow puts herself forward as leader. I stare at her, she stares at me, eventually I moo in her face, before a farmer appears and goes apeshit. Between Helston and Porthleven and Mullion takes me past 500 miles, and every message I read that night is like a power pill, the side effect being they make me teary: I don't know most of these people, and they're being so, so kind.

I'm full of cold after a soaking in Saltash, but just have to man up and plough through it. Heidi from Mounts Bay Harriers runs her first marathon, over part of the Classic Quarter course from Lizard to Land's End, and what an achievement that is. At one point, I slip and almost topple over a cliff; at another, we're literally scrabbling up a hill on all fours; and after I descend the steps from the Minack Theatre onto Porthcurno Beach, a death-defying feat in itself, I discover we've covered 11 miles in four and a half hours. But who's really counting? With its golden sand and crystal blue waters, we could have been on a Greek island. Three hours later, we're at Land's End, and I think to myself: 'Right, I'm at one end of the country, and now the other end of the country seems so far away.' Reaching Land's End didn't feel like the triumphant moment I thought it might, it just made the goal seem further away than ever.

I get lost again in Redruth on day 24, where I am on my own for the second time, but two laps of the beautiful Cornish village of Indian Queens the following day are the perfect pick-me-up. Three members of Newquay Road Runners knock out distance PBs, and it's becoming increasingly apparent that people are feeding off my strength and confidence and pushing their own limits. Just as important, people online are finding their voice, sending me messages about the bullying they've been through, which is exactly the point. I don't just want to shine a light on bullying, I want people to talk about it and not feel ashamed, like I felt for so long, before kicking on and accomplishing things they had never even dreamed of.

Day 27 in Launceston is pretty much the perfect day, and I'll miss Cornwall and its immense generosity. Having put me up in the grounds of her house, the lovely Lucy cooks me a fry-up, before sending me on my way. Out on the course, 27 members of Launceston Road Runners plod along with me, together with members of clubs throughout Cornwall, and it's the biggest turnout to date. At the 11-mile mark, Joss opens up her house and serves up pasties, tea and cake.

Nine of the runners set new PBs, including a few who completed marathons having had absolutely no intention of doing so. This is starting to happen a lot, I think because people are getting carried away with the magic of the Challenge. It's nice that they wanted to run with me and support me and what we were trying to achieve, but it can get overwhelming at times. So it's also nice to be the guy at the back, geeing other people up and setting targets. I've got good at selecting one person in the group who I'll persuade to run a marathon with me. Gently, of course. At the start of every day, I'll say: 'So, how far is everyone thinking of running?' And it's often the people who say, 'Oh, I don't know, I've just come out for a bit of fun', that are still there at the finish line. Seeing the look in somebody's eyes after they've achieved something that wasn't even on their radar that morning makes me quite emotional and is starting to become addictive.

* * * * * * * * * *

Paula Radcliffe, marathon world record holder: *Ben didn't seem to think that what he was doing was a big deal. Talk to him and he'd be like: 'I honestly haven't done much, I had a lot of help and support.' He was right to thank his support team, they were amazing – and I'll never forget my physio, Gerard Hartmann, who treated me twice a day when I ran 151 miles in a week – but Ben was the beating heart of it.*

He was very smart in the way he structured the Challenge. He got clubs involved, had people out running with him every day, ran with kids, stopped for lunch. When I trained, I trained for quality. But what Ben was trying to do was different in so many ways. He was just trying to get round each day. And it doesn't matter if you eat cake and drink coffee on the way round – whatever gets you through it, and it's still a marathon if you run 26.2 miles! The upshot was that every day was broken down into smaller chunks. That made it easier physically, but also mentally.

* * * * * * * * * *

Almost as soon as I moved into my new flat in Portishead, having separated from my wife, I started plastering the bedroom walls with flip-chart paper and writing down anything that came into my head. I was like Russell Crowe in *A Beautiful Mind*, maniacal, verging on psychotic. It was as if I'd thrown the workings of my brain onto that wall and was trying to work myself out mathematically. There were numbers, spider diagrams, drawings and scribbles, and my task was to work out the puzzle.

In the beginning, there was a lot of gibberish, including things I thought I wanted, but later worked out I didn't. It was a case of sifting through the chaos and picking out the truth. Because I was now on my own, I was independent, so able to focus purely on me. The process lasted for about three months. The breakthrough came when I started writing down what a happy life would look like. Now, it wasn't a case of picking out the truth, the truth just came pouring out. My job required me to spend a lot of time on the road, and I fantasised about this other life I wanted while I was driving. Suddenly, all those fantasies and dreams took centre stage: to love a man, and have a man love me; to be happy with a man; to know the feel of a man; to feel safe with a man; to walk along the beach with a man; to have a dog together. All things I hadn't thought possible, because of what I thought society expected of me.

. . . .

When kids started calling me gay at school, I didn't have a clue what gay was, except that it was meant to be wrong. And I didn't want to be wrong, I just wanted to be like everybody else. I knew I was different from when I was about 13, but didn't really know how. I found boys attractive and masculinity attractive in men, but I wasn't attracted to girls or effeminate boys. I buried it for a couple of years, until I was 14 or 15, when I finally realised what I was. Even then, I only thought I was gay because people were calling me gay, that's how messed up my head was. I can't remember how I figured it out, but when I did, it scared me.

There's a lot more awareness nowadays, but there was no information when I was at school. I had nobody to discuss it with, and I just assumed that everybody, even the teachers, thought being gay was a bad thing to be. It seemed really odd that that's what I could be. I remember going home to Mum and Dad's in Lincoln, going on the computer and looking at images of gay porn. I was absolutely petrified, thinking: 'Oh no, this can't be it, they must have all this wrong...' I didn't know anything about clearing browser history, so Dad discovered all these images of naked men, and men having sex with other men. He marched me and my brother downstairs, plonked us on the sofa and read us the riot act: 'Why are you looking at this type of material? It's disgraceful!' Later, I realised he wasn't angry because it was gay material, he was just angry because it was pornographic.

So I went back to school and wrote a letter to my parents, telling them – categorically, without any shadow of a doubt, 100 per cent – that I was not gay. I was just so scared of what people might think if they knew the truth. If anything, I protested too much but it seemed to do the trick. I'd dodged a bullet and my secret was still under wraps. Looking back, I wish my parents had worked out that the vehemence of my denials was proof of a cover-up.

* * * * * * * * * *

Beverley Smith, Ben's mum: *When that letter arrived, I rang Pete immediately and said: 'We've got to go and see Ben, something's going on at school.' On arrival, I said to Ben: 'Whatever's going on, darling? It doesn't matter to us if you're gay, you'll be our son whatever.' The other kids had been taunting him because he was so soft and gentle. But he didn't* *want to tell us about it because he didn't want us to feel guilty. He saw how upset I got when they went away, so that was him being the grown-up little boy, brave for his daddy and trying not to worry me. He repeated everything he'd written in the letter, insisted he wasn't gay, and that was the last we heard about his sexuality for about 16 years. But the bullying never stopped.*

The day after we found him in the garage, I took him to the doctor and she was just wonderful. I stepped out of the room and left them to talk, and Ben must have opened up to her. She wrote a letter to the headmaster, telling him that this young man would be better off never returning to his school. We got Ben a private tutor, so he could continue with his A-levels at home. But he wasn't in a fit state to do anything, let alone study.

. . . .

After leaving school, I went to study at Teesside University in Middlesbrough, because that's what I thought I was supposed to do. I'd had so much of the stuffing knocked out of me, I didn't know who I was or what my place in the world was, so I went to university because everybody else was doing it. The only reason I studied what I did was because Mum was a counsellor at the time and said: 'Why don't you do psychology?' And I said: 'Oh, alright then.' Bear in mind I'm dyslexic, and I chose a subject which required me to read a shit-load of books and write lots of essays. Madness.

Just like when I went from prep to senior school, I thought everything might suddenly be different when I went to university. People often talk about uni as the place where they 'find' or 'regenerate' themselves, where they learn to stand on their own two feet, finally blossom or emerge from their chrysalis. But although the environment allowed that, I didn't allow myself to change. I was conditioned to be a certain way, all that bullying at school had had such a profound effect on me. I was completely broken, no more than a shell. I didn't have the confidence, energy or ability to be reimagining myself.

In my first term I tried to take my own life again. After a very drunken night out at the Students' Union, I went back to my room, locked the door and took a mixture of 30 paracetamol and aspirin, with the intention of not waking up. Two hours later, I was bent over in intense pain, throwing up in the sink. When I eventually emerged from my room a couple of days later, the girl next door asked if I was alright. I told her what I'd done and ended up in hospital. They fitted me to a drip that made my kidneys hurt – imagine really wanting to pee, multiplied by about 20 – and rather than being supportive, the nurses treated me as if I was a loser, wasting their time. I had my obligatory 15-minute appointment with a shrink, faked it again and was given a clean bill of health – I don't even remember what he said.

That second time was a cry for help: I just wanted someone to hug me and tell me everything was going to be OK, but nobody did. The nurses didn't care, the shrink didn't care, and I had nobody else to turn to. That was the point when I thought: 'I've tried to kill myself twice, haven't been successful, so I might as well just exist.'

When I did make a tentative attempt to be the real me, I was punched in the stomach, albeit not literally. A girl on my course had quite a lot of gay friends, and I felt comfortable talking to her. So one night, I plucked up the courage and told her I thought I was gay. But she didn't hug or congratulate me, but said: 'Are you sure your housemates want to live with a gay person?' She was the first person I'd told, and that was the reaction. The following morning, I retracted my story and told her I'd made a mistake, which made it twice I'd climbed back into the closet. Shortly after that, I was in my bedroom after a drunken evening, in a desperate, depressed state, and I could hear the girl in the front room, telling everybody I was gay. Seconds later, they were all banging on my door, taunting me, with one guy shouting in a camp voice: 'Just let me in, Ben, I'm obviously what you want!' I felt utterly victimised. What that girl did to me was absolutely despicable, especially considering that she knew about my suicide attempt. No wonder it took me so long to come out again.

I soon lost interest in the course, stopped attending lectures and, for whatever reason, that frustrated my housemates. I'd set up all the bills and the girls I lived with weren't pitching in, so I was left out of pocket. Dad got involved and it all got very messy. In the end, I absolutely lost it and moved in with the girl who had told everyone I was gay. That was the only place I could go, I had no other options. That's how friendless I was.

In my second year I took a year out and worked at a disabilities camp in America. But even out there I played another version of myself, going along with all that bravado around the campfire. I became over-confident to compensate for my lack of confidence, which I'm quite ashamed of. Now, when I see that kind of over-confidence in other people, I sometimes wonder what they're hiding, deep inside. While I was there, I started a relationship with a girl from the UK, which carried on for a while when we returned to the UK, until I made the decision to end it.

As time went on, my focus became clubbing, drinking, smoking and taking drugs. After I graduated, I chose to stay in Middlesbrough, where I'd come under the influence of a group of supposed friends. I threw myself headlong into these drug-fuelled nights of escapism, which involved taking anything I could get my hands on. It was my way of escaping, leaving all the shit behind. I'd completely lost control again. I didn't have an anchor, and when people aren't anchored they can drift into rocky waters. In a way I enjoyed it, because it meant I didn't have to be me and everybody was the same when we were all off our faces.

My eyes were opened to things I'd never seen before – drug dealing, prostitution, violence. I was at parties where people overdosed on ketamine. But even though there was a gay club on the high street, and part of me wanted to go, I didn't feel like I could – I'd pushed things down so deep, I'd almost started believing that I was this role I was playing.

I got a job at Topman and worked in bars, on the promotions and marketing side of things, but that just meant I had money to spend on the wrong things. This had never been my life: I had a nice upbringing, but I felt grown-up in that environment and as if nobody could get to me. But after becoming far too partial to pills and getting into a lot of debt because of a growing coke habit, I had the good sense to stop. I've always had this little person on one shoulder, telling me when I've gone too far. It was after he had one of his little chats with me that I decided to move home.

CHAPTER 6

Is That It?

Three or four months after returning to Lincoln, I met the woman who would become my wife. Because I'd been working at Topman in Middlesbrough, and my cousin was one of their learning and development officers, I was encouraged to apply for a place on their graduate programme. I was offered a placement and my first post was deputy manager at Topman in the Gateshead Metro Centre, working under a lovely lady called Heather. I then had spells in Newcastle, London and Nottingham, before me and my future wife decided to move to the South West, where she had landed a new job.

In Bristol, I got a job as operations manager at the new Topshop and Topman store in Cabot Circus shopping centre. Six months later I left and got a job with a large corporate FTSE 100 company. A few years passed and we decided to move from Bristol to Portishead and rented a house before taking the leap a year later and bought a four-bedroomed house in Portishead. I was on a lot of money compared to what I had been earning before, which included previously unimaginable bonuses, so it looked like I had the dream – big bucks, big house, big car, pension plan, two holidays a year, a lovely girlfriend. But I felt empty inside. I got very good at faking contentment, had created my own warped reality, my own screwed-up set of beliefs, so nobody knew otherwise. By then, I'd had a lot of practice in lying.

You know what happened next, and separating from my wife was the catalyst I needed. I no longer had anything to lose, I felt uncluttered, and I decided I wasn't going to be that person anymore. In my bedroom, surrounded by my dreams, which had been whittled down and refined over the weeks, I finally decided I'd done enough planning and it was time to go out and be me, starting with my sexuality. It took me a while to pluck up the courage to sign up to gay dating app Grindr. I'd never kissed a man or even held a man's hand before, and I was 31.

The first time I had sex with a man was in Helsinki, when I was over there for a marathon in 2014. He was an Englishman, a lot younger than me, and it felt right. It wasn't some monumental moment, it just confirmed something I already knew: 'Yeah, I was right, let's move on.' I was self-conscious, a bit embarrassed, because I was in my 30s and I didn't know what I was supposed to be doing. In a gay relationship, I had the added complication of figuring out what my preferences were and what role I was going to play. With women, I knew what I was supposed to be doing; with men, it was a little bit more complex. It was like being a teenager all over again. The difference this time was that I had this new-found vigour, and I was doing it while being who I really was.

The great thing about doing all those marathons in far-flung places was that I was only there for the weekend, so I could hook up on Grindr and I was never going to see them again. It gave me the freedom to figure out what I wanted, without any fallout so I took every opportunity I could in every city I ran in to try things out. A big part of attraction is the confidence someone has, which suggests they know who they are. Because I now knew who I was, I felt more attractive, and I was playing catch-up. Even when I had something close to a relationship with a guy in Bristol, we weren't exclusive, and it just cemented in my mind that I was too old to carry on like that. Grindr is a very convenient tool, but it's basically about sex. And having made up for lost time and had fun doing it, I was beginning to work out what type of a man and relationship I wanted.

SEPTEMBER 2015 IN NUMBERS
Marathons: **30**
Miles run: **799** (average per day: **26.6**)
Running time: **161:51.35** hours (average per day: **5:23.43**)
Number of people run with: **250**
Distance personal bests: **16**
First marathons/ultra-marathons: **6**
Pints of cider: **16**
Flat whites: **30**

DAYS 28–47: Devon and Cornwall are wonderful, but absolutely exhausting. I'm driving on bad roads, getting up at six, introducing myself to new people, answering questions, going for massage therapy, updating social media, and obviously running the odd marathon. On the video message I record in Bude, where I pass the 750-mile mark, I look and sound terrible. Some nights I'll have a cry in the van, because I'm so tired and trying to function in the most basic way. Whenever that happens, I'll look in the mirror, see myself crying and say: 'What the fuck is wrong with you? Pull yourself together, man!'

. . . .

28 MARATHONS DOWN – JUST THE 373 TO GO FOR FUNDRAISER

WESTERN DAILY PRESS, 28 SEPTEMBER 2015

'…During the first 25 marathons Ben has had to come to terms with some miserable weather and tough hills. He told his fans he had been suffering with tendonitis in his left shin but that it was improving…'

. . . .

At the Bournemouth Marathon on day 34, my first official marathon of the Challenge, I somehow crank out a time of 3 hours, 55 minutes. I've no idea where that time came from – my average time before then had been about 5 hours, 20 minutes – but I just flew. I pass 900 miles in Christchurch the following day, accompanied by Danny, dressed in a Spider-Man onesie on a bike. We got some looks, especially because it was absolutely tipping it down. Around the 21-mile mark we celebrate with a cheeky can of Thatchers and some Jaffa Cakes – which I have quickly worked out are the cider and cakes of choice for marathon runners.

Passing through Southampton and on to Eastleigh for day 38, it is all about The Two Jims – one of whom had already run about 140 marathons, while the other completed his first with me. The Stubbington Green Runners, the largest group to turn out so far, lead me through the 1000-mile mark on day 39, and bizarrely, I stay at Stephen Fry's husband's parents' house, although I don't know who they are until they tell me over dinner, when I almost spit my chicken out. It was they who told Stephen what I was doing, hence the supportive tweet a week or so earlier.

After Stubbington, I make my way to Portsmouth, where I meet up with the local running club and take part in the first parkrun of the Challenge. Next, it's over on the ferry for the Isle of Wight Marathon on day 41, back to Portsmouth, on to Hayling Island for day 43 and out onto the South Downs Way. It's a whirlwind, and while I wouldn't say I'm losing motivation, I have to admit I'm flagging. Some mornings I wake up and have no idea how many marathons I've run, which means I have no idea how many marathons I have left, and I'm not sure if that's a good thing. Then, coming up to the 50-day mark, my body suddenly falls into a groove. It's as if it has said to itself: 'Right, clearly nagging's not going to work, might as well just get on with it.' Nobody said this was going to happen, although, to be fair, I'm not sure anybody could have told me, even if I'd asked.

* * * * * * * * * *

I had no advice from medical people beforehand, simply because I couldn't afford it. We contacted universities and health professionals and there were a couple of people who took an initial interest, but they soon went off the idea. The 401 team and I got a bit sick of people letting us down, so decided we'd just work it out ourselves as we went along. The lack of interest was probably a blessing in disguise. If I'd had a medical advisor following me around all the time, I don't think I would have done it, because they would have told me to stop at the first sign of danger. And I'm not sure a nutritionist could have helped anyway, because nobody in the UK had ever done anything on this scale before, at least not to our knowledge. Therefore, there were no rules.

For the first 50 days, I stuck to what I thought were the basics, as laid out in magazines I'd read, in terms of eating the recommended number of calories a day for an endurance runner and loading up on carbohydrates and supplements. I'd eat a bowl of porridge for breakfast, snack on nuts, and consume lots of rice and potatoes for energy. I'm not a massive fan of pasta, but I didn't really have a choice, because whenever I stayed with people I ate whatever was put in front of me, and pasta was almost always what I was given. They'd been kind enough to cook for me and put me up for the night, so it's not like I was going to complain! But because I was eating mainly carbs, I felt full, but I was actually not eating enough and running on a calorie deficit a lot of the time. I lost 17kg over those first 50 days, dropped to 70kg, and my body fat was as low as 7 per cent at one point. My insides felt cold and achy, as if somebody was punching me, because the visceral fat around my organs had wasted away to almost nothing. I felt sick and low on energy, my body was absolutely shot after every marathon. And because I had no energy and my brain wasn't being fed either, my motivation was dwindling.

So eventually I decided I was going to do what I wanted to do and stop doing the 'right' thing. I love food and I love coffee, so I worked it into my daily planning. I'd run eight miles, stop off at a café and have a flat white, because that was what motivated me. I started eating higher-fat, higher-protein food, because that was what I craved. The first time I stopped for a burger, it sent pure, fatty energy coursing through my veins. That felt so good! I'd stop off for fish and chips, roast dinners, whatever I could get into me, because that's what I felt like eating at that time. My breakfasts became famous, huge portions of eggs, bacon, hash browns – complete madness in some people's eyes. I'd also have a pint of cider almost every day. Imagine Paula Radcliffe or Mo Farah stopping off for a pint halfway round a marathon! Any nutritionist worth their salt would have been telling me: 'You've got to eat this, you've got to eat that, you can't be eating this.' But I'm not an elite athlete, I was just an ordinary bloke, doing something out of the ordinary, so maybe the rules were different for me. As one leading nutritionist pointed out to me after the Challenge, what I was doing was probably *beyond* elite, in that it had never really been done before.

I'd been sold this idea of needing to eat 'healthy' food, until I worked out that my body was constantly in fight mode, just trying to survive, so it just needed anything I could get my hands on, in whatever quantity. So when my intuition told me I needed a burger,

I stopped and had one. My energy levels shot right up, my body fat increased, my weight stabilised and my injuries stopped. As a result of all that, I got my motivation back. So, if anyone out there is thinking of running 401 marathons, my first piece of advice would be: 'Bacon and egg sandwiches all the way!'

. . . .

After a few experiences with men, I decided to tell my friend Susan that I was gay. We were in the front room of my flat and it took me about 15 minutes to get it out. When I finally did, she said: 'Oh, is that it? I thought you were going to tell me you had cancer.' And she carried on eating her risotto. What she *didn't* say was: 'Yeah, I already knew that.' Nobody seemed to know. I was like: 'Seriously? Come on! Really?' And they'd say: 'Not a fucking clue.' I hid it well, then. The fact that Susan was so blasé about it gave me the strength to tell another friend, so we broke it to Laura together on a flight to Seville. Laura, who has an incredibly dry sense of humour, was like: 'Oh, OK. Happy days!' And then the jokes started coming out. It was their way of saying: 'You know what? We really don't give a shit.' It was amazing!

Telling Mum and Dad was a little bit different. It normally takes three and a half hours to drive up from Bristol to Lincoln, but this time it took me eight. I stopped at every service station along the way and must have got through at least 40 fags (I was still smoking, despite running marathons). I was sitting in my car, dragging on a cigarette, rehearsing my speech, wondering what the reaction would be. When I finally arrived, Dad was on the phone to my brother, Dan, who had just got his first job after retiring as a professional rugby player, selling beer for Peroni. That was a big deal for him, but I was sitting on the kitchen table, swinging my legs, thinking: 'Please just get off the phone…'

When Dad was done, I took them through to the lounge and said: 'I've got something to tell you.' Fifteen minutes later, I still hadn't told them. It was just so big, it got stuck on the way out. Eventually it came: 'I think I might be gay.' I didn't say 'I was gay', I said 'I might be gay', because that gave me a way out. Dad looked at me and said, in his usual Dad way: 'Are you happy?' 'Yeah, I really am,' I said. And he said: 'Well, alright then.' Mum burst into tears, gave me a big hug and said: 'We'll love you no matter what.' She and Dad should write a manual on how to react when your son or daughter comes out, it was pretty much perfect. The next words out of Dad's mouth were: 'Shall we go and get some fish and chips?' The biggest thing I will ever tell my parents and that was his reaction! After telling me, in a joking way of course, that I wasn't allowed to wear her shoes, Mum texted my brother, and he texted back saying: 'You've gone and topped me again, you bastard. I get a bloody job and you come out with that!' A minute later he texted again: 'I'm proud of you and love you.'

That was that. You build these things up so that they seem monumentally important, because you've been ashamed of who you really are for so long, and there will be millions of people all over the world right now stuck in the same situation as I was. It might not be the same for everyone, but when I came out, I discovered that nobody really gave a shit. That was probably the best night's sleep I ever had. But even better was waking up the following morning, looking in the mirror and knowing I didn't need to put that fake face on ever again.

* * * * * * * * * *

Pete Smith, Ben's dad: *When he told us he was gay, I said: 'So, what's the important thing you've come to tell us about? It doesn't bloody matter!' He's our Ben, he'll always be our Ben.*

I was just upset that he'd been trapped in that other world for so long, because of what he thought other people expected of him. Isn't it awful that society can drive a person down a route that's just not for them?

Beverley Smith, Ben's mum: *The first thing we knew about him being gay was when he was sat on the settee after his marriage had broken down and he finally decided to tell us. We had no inkling, none whatsoever. He'd had girlfriends, he'd been married and lived with her for years before that. We were disappointed he felt he couldn't tell us, but what really hurt us was that someone we loved and cared for so preciously had been forced to live a life he didn't want to be living.*

· · · · · · · · · ·

I don't know why I had worried about it so much – I think it was more about whether I was *ready* to tell them, rather than being worried about how they would react. My relationship with Mum and Dad was always strong, other than when I was with my wife. So while I don't think coming out necessarily made our relationship stronger, it meant they got to know the real me for the first time.

Dad is military through and through, but he's not a classic, buttoned-up type. He'll talk at me sometimes rather than to me, but that's what dads do, and he's been barking orders for 40 years. But he managed through respect rather than fear, and he wouldn't ask you to do something he wouldn't do himself. Like most dads he thinks he knows everything and is a man of specifics. I could say: 'This cup is green.' And he'd say: 'No, it's not. I think you'll find it's luminous green.' I love the fact that, even if he gets the specifics completely wrong, he has the audacity to stand his ground, at the same time as

I'm thinking: 'You're talking bollocks, Dad.' He's a loving father, very wise, very open-minded, would do anything for anybody, and I love him to death.

Dad has seen things not many people have seen and that must put life into perspective. He doesn't talk much about his time in the RAF. He's a proud man and wants to be the person with all the problems, so that nobody else has any. I can see how much some of what he experienced troubles him sometimes, but he loved his job all the same. It's ironic, because if I had just taken more notice of him when I was younger, I would have learned that finding what makes you happy is what life should be about. Dad wanted to be in the RAF from when he was a kid and that's what he ended up doing. But when you're young you don't necessarily want to see your Mum and Dad for who they really are, and I didn't live with them anyway for many years. Maybe because of that, I didn't have a great relationship with Dad until my late teens. Now, we're closer than ever. He's one of the most wonderful people I know.

Mum is a mother hen and the person who held the household together. Dad would turn up and say: 'Sorry, I'm disappearing for three months, I can't really tell you where I'm going.' When I lived at home after leaving university, Dad was in the Falklands, and Mum and I would watch *CSI* together when she couldn't sleep, with a plate of chicken wings. It was our quality time and I think she cherished those times as much as I did. Mum knew the score with Dad's job, because she was a nurse in the RAF when she met him. She would do anything for her family and is very loyal and honest. She'll also tell her whole life story to strangers, which is obviously where I get it from. After finishing nursing, she set up her own counselling business, and after Grandma died, she set up a bereavement counselling charity. She believes in a more spiritual plan, something I always respected but struggled to understand.

One day she announced that she wanted to be a medium and me and Dad just looked at each other, eyebrows raised.

Mum and Dad are opposite ends of the scale in some ways – Mum is very holistic, Dad is very black and white and logical, and I'm both of them mixed up together. Maybe this is the secret to running 401 marathons in 401 days?! They are absolute soulmates, more in love now than they've ever been, and I'm so lucky to have them as parents.

My relationship with my brother suffered when I went away to boarding school, when I was 10 and he was six. Because Mum had been told she couldn't have kids, when I came along they maybe coddled me a little too much, because they wanted to protect me. And because I wasn't strong enough to deal with my own bullying, when Dan joined me at secondary school I couldn't protect him and be the big brother he was used to. I don't know if he blames me, but I know he had a shit time at school. I'm sure there was an element of embarrassment that his older brother was being bullied, and because he was my younger brother, he got tarred with the same brush and started taking flak himself. Once he was taken out of school, he flourished. He was always sportier than me, grew into a big unit of a man and became a professional rugby player. But, looking back, I don't think we were as different as it seemed at the time. I remember wanting to do GCSE PE, but my parents said to me: 'No, that's what your brother does.' That's almost the way it had to be: Dan was the sporty one, I was the sensitive one. But we both could have been sporty – if I'd kept up swimming, I reckon I could have been pretty good at it – and it's taken us all these years to realise that we're a lot more similar than we ever thought we were.

. . . .

Dan Smith, Ben's brother: *Ben and I were really close as children. We'd always be out on our bikes, or spending hours together on our pedal go-karts, adventuring and exploring. I have vivid memories of our time in Germany. I remember playing in the front garden, wearing matching outfits, and these massive army tanks coming down our road and parking outside our house. We would climb this big cherry tree after dinner, sit in the branches, eat cherries, spit the pips out and chat. I also remember him throwing a firecracker at my head at one of Mum and Dad's New Year's Eve parties, and me being the one who got in trouble. He was a mischievous little shit at times, although, truth be told, we were both as bad as each other. But we were also best mates.*

Before he went off to boarding school, I remember him packing his bags with Mum, and I could see he was nervous. I cried in my bedroom, because I was worried for him and didn't want to be without my best mate. Things were never the same from that point on. Not long after Ben left for boarding school, I followed, because I wouldn't stop pestering my poor mum and dad to send me. I just wanted to be with my big brother. Ben helped me through the early weeks, but he was having a challenging time himself, and wasn't the same brother I knew from home. I couldn't do anything to help because I was only nine, and although it wasn't his fault and there was nothing he could have done, I became guilty by association. I ended up being bullied myself, although nowhere near as badly as Ben, and this put a strain on our relationship. We both needed each other, but because we were young and didn't really understand what was happening, we grew further and further apart.

When I followed him to secondary school, Ben was having a particularly bad time of things. But I didn't really appreciate how bad it was, because we only saw each other every now and again in passing. I was getting bullied as well, mainly verbally, although there was one time I had my shirt super-glued to my back. But for Ben, the bullying was on another level. Some Sundays, when things were really bad for me, I would go to Ben's room and play on the computer for hours. It was a safe haven, but we never really talked about what was happening. We were just trying to survive. Bullying changed Ben, it changed me, and it changed our relationship completely.

• • • • • • • • • •

DAY 48: In Eastbourne, after a shot of muscle activation therapy, which is basically doing an awful lot of stretching, I feel like I can run and run and never stop running. I almost feel guilty because I'm having a whale of a time, doing what I want to be doing and absolutely loving it. I feel like it should be more difficult, and sometimes I think: 'Does this look too easy? Do I need to make it look tougher?!'

CHAPTER 7

The Perfect Partner

Having had my fill of Grindr, I registered for another dating app called Plenty of Fish, which seemed a bit more my style. One night in December 2014, I was sitting on my sofa with a friend, absent-mindedly swiping through profiles, when I first came across Kyle's profile. As soon as I saw him, I thought: '*Hello…*' I just knew. He was stocky and masculine and covered in tattoos, all of which I find attractive. I read his profile – which you don't tend to do on Grindr – and we had the same morals and values. I'd been compiling lists of things I wanted in a partner, and he pretty much ticked off all of them. So I thought: 'Hey, let's give this a go.' I liked his picture and he sent a message straight back saying: 'Let's go on a date.' I was shit-ting myself, thinking: 'Fuck! What have I done? I'm not good enough for you. How the hell do you like me? This must be some kind of mistake!'

When he told me he was moving from Bournemouth, where he was doing his PhD, to Bristol the very next day, it just felt like everything had suddenly aligned. For our first date, I picked him up from his flat and took him out for breakfast in Portishead, before we went for a walk on Sandy Bay, just north of Weston-super-Mare. He'd recently had an operation on his feet and was still recovering, so I chose the beach as it would be easier for him to walk. What a gentleman! After I'd dropped him off at his flat, I immediately wanted to see him again. I'd fallen for him, big style. He was all I could think about. When I told him about The 401 Challenge on our first date, he just said: 'That sounds quite good.' That made me like him even more, because it was the craziest possible thing I could come up with and it didn't faze him one bit.

* * * * * * * * * *

Kyle Waters, Ben's partner: *Ben viewed my profile a couple of times online so in the end I sent him a message. I just said: 'I don't want to waste time messaging back and forth, here's my number.' What attracted me to him was the fact he was a typical bloke, and I mean that in a nice way. He was just a normal guy doing normal things, at least that's what I thought! I'd just had some metal pins taken out of my feet, so we went for a little walk on the beach. He told me about the Challenge, and it became clear that on top of being a normal guy doing normal things, he was an amazing person who wanted to do amazing things. You can be both. I didn't think he was crazy, I wasn't fazed by it at all. It's great to have goals, great to have unwavering belief. So I just said: 'OK, that's amazing, I hope you do it.' And I knew he would, I believed in him from the very start.*

It was his confidence that persuaded me, the way he talked about it in a very matter-of-fact way: 'I am going to do this thing and I am going to be successful.' I had a feeling things must have happened in his life to make him want to do the Challenge and after a couple of dates he told me about the bullying. I was bullied, too, but wasn't affected by it like he was. His experience was a lot worse, and I was always able to tell myself that the bullies weren't going to be as successful in life as me. But I've never known the old Ben, the Ben that I fell in love with was very different. Even when he told me the stories, it was like he was talking about a different person. But what happened to him at school made him the amazing man he is today, doing the amazing things he's doing. It was a traumatic time for him, but he can't regret it too much. Without that time, he would be living a completely different life.

My mum and dad met Ben after about a month of me living in Bristol and they loved him straightaway. I think they liked the fact he was just a normal man who happened to be gay, he wasn't defined by his sexuality. He fitted into my life and I fitted into his. I went on holiday for two weeks just before he started the Challenge, and I was doing my archaeology PhD at the same time. We had to spend weeks and weeks apart, which was challenging, but we could deal with it. In fact, I think it just made the relationship stronger.

· · · · · · · · · ·

We saw each other again on New Year's Day and Kyle soon became my first proper boyfriend. It was all my fantasies starting to come true and I felt so relieved that it didn't feel weird or unnatural. Remember how it feels falling in love, then imagine how it feels falling in love when you never thought it could happen. I'd never believed that old saying, 'When you know, you know', but you do. It hits you like a freight train and you don't know whether you're coming or going. You can grab hold of it and ride it, or you can try to fight it. I'd been fighting it for too many years, so I grabbed hold of it. Although I waited until the second date. As I said, I'm a gentleman.

I didn't think he had fallen as hard for me as I fell for him, but it still felt right. Quite early on, Kyle said: 'I'm not going to tell you I love you for the first three months.' He lasted a month and a half. When he told me, I said: 'I'm so glad you said that, because I've been wanting to say it ever since I met you.' I'd been through all that shit and now I was rewarded with the one thing I'd always wanted in life – the perfect partner. And when I say, 'the perfect partner', this is a guy who doesn't share my passion for running. In fact, he hates it. And I was about to start running 401 marathons. And he was doing his PhD at the time. And he was off on holiday to Australia two days before the Challenge started. He'd booked it before we got together, and when he said he didn't have to go, I told him not to be silly.

All in all, it was like some weird relationship test gameshow. I dropped him off on his birthday – 29 August – and I cried when I said goodbye to him, because I was worried we wouldn't be able to make it last. I'd finally found this perfect man I'd been looking for, and now I was pissing off for 401 days. I did feel guilty, but he could see how important it was to me. And maybe it was a blessing in disguise. We're both quite independent, so don't need to be in each other's pockets all the time, and him not being there gave me the space to be able to focus on the project. He stuck by me and gave me the freedom to go away and follow my dream, and you can't ask for much more than that.

* * * * * * * * * *

Beverley Smith, Ben's mum: *Once he came out, he was our Ben again – you could see that light in his eyes he used to have as a kid and his strength came back to him. When he met Kyle, he phoned me and said: 'Oh Mum, I've met this lovely, amazing fella.' I said: 'Fill your boots, you lucky bugger!' He's been shining ever since. And when they're together, the shine comes off the both of them. You can tell Kyle loves Ben, loves the bones of him. Ben said that when he*

*first introduced us, he might be a bit quiet. But we shared a
bottle of Prosecco and we've been best of mates ever since.
Even when Ben visits on his own, and even if he's tired or
stressed, you get him talking about Kyle and his eyes light
up again.*

• • • • • • • • • •

DAY 49: My first school visit of the Challenge is in Battle, Sussex,
and I absolutely love it. I could just visit schools and talk about my
experiences for the rest of my life. School visits were always part
of the plan, but nothing was in place before I set off. So organising
the visits has become part of Tolu and Kyle's remit (on top of
everything else!). As the Challenge progresses, the visits become
absolutely integral to the project, and it gets to the point where
people are asking us to visit schools, rather than the other way
round. I did my university dissertation on bullying, and as part of
my research I spoke to groups of kids in schools. But that was very
different to talking in front of a whole school. The first few times
during the Challenge, I'm really nervous – especially standing in
front of a room full of teenagers who all think I'm nuts – because
I don't really know what I'm going to say. But what I say goes
down well, and I've got time to work out what has worked and
what hasn't.

I don't have a preference between primary or secondary, it's just two
different versions of the same story. With the younger kids, it's about
putting my story into context. I don't talk about my sexuality or suicide
attempts because it isn't appropriate for kids of that age. I get kids who
want to know what my favourite pizza topping is, kids who want to know
if I've been running with a bulldog. All the really important questions!
The craziest things come out of their mouths, but they're excited and

engaged. I tell them I've run however many times around their playground, or from where they're sitting to Sydney, and they can't get their heads around it.

Then we talk about why I'm doing the Challenge. I ask if they know what bullying is and how it makes them feel, and usually they answer in one word. And some of those words are very profound – 'suicide', 'depressed', 'anxious'. I even had a five-year-old use the word 'melancholy'. And then I say: 'What if I told you I was bullied for eight years and all those words you just said are how it made me feel?' I've had a few kids stand up and tell the entire school they're being bullied, which is a huge thing to do. I'd talk to them afterwards, with a teacher, to make sure they were OK. Then, I like to lighten things up again with a few stories about pizza toppings and running with dogs!

. . . .

Stefanie Beamish-Pena, an inspired teacher: *I read Ben's story on the Run Mummy Run website and found it very inspirational. At the time, I was teaching at St Michael's Easthampstead Primary School in Bracknell, and I just dropped him an email, asking if he'd be happy to come and talk to our children and tell them what he was up to. I didn't really know how he would be with the kids, but I guessed that somebody who was willing to do 401 marathons for such good causes would definitely inspire them. And from a purely selfish point of view, I was just desperate to meet him, as were other members of staff.*

He was such a nice guy and we all fell in love with him. Some people can stand in front of an audience and grab their attention. He was one of those people, almost hypnotic. He was talking to children as young as four and a half, but you could see on their faces how excited they were. They asked really odd questions, like: 'Have you run with penguins?' They were also obsessed with how many medals he had, because they thought he won one after every marathon. He was able to put things into the kids' language, like when he told them how many times he'd run around their playground. I was watching him speak and thinking: 'He's had such a hard life, how does he keep smiling?' So many people just sit on their problems and feel sorry for themselves.

When he talked about bullying, which is obviously a serious subject, he pitched it just right. His message was positive: if you want something, go for it, there's nothing to lose; work hard for what you want; don't listen to what anybody else says. Some kids don't hear those kinds of positive messages in their homes and need that confidence boost. The fact that they were hearing it from somebody who had done this amazing thing made it even more valuable. Ben wasn't doing 401 marathons because he thought it made him sound cool, he was doing it for what he believed in.

The whole day ended on a high, everybody was just so happy. He was like a fluffy cloud of happiness floating into the school, raining glitter. All the women had a huge crush on him. And I wanted him to be my friend: 'Please don't go!' It was one of the highlights of the year, for me and for the school. I hope I can be like Ben, contribute to society and bring people together. You don't have to run 401 marathons, but you do have to find your niche.

* * * * * * * * * *

In Stroud, the local BBC come along to do some filming at a school I'm giving a talk at. This little kid, who can't be more than four years old, puts his hand up and is really straining as if he wants to ask the most important question in the world. I say: 'What's your question?' And he says, after a little deliberation: 'I need a wee.' The teachers' heads drop and the cameraman's shoulders start moving up and down, because it was just so unexpected and funny. That teaches me not to plan anything too much, to just enjoy it, because it will probably all go to pot anyway. But because I have respect for the kids, and talk to them rather than down to them, they engage. And hopefully, by the time I've finished, they'll be inspired to do something amazing.

Secondary school kids I can be a bit more raw with. I tell them about having a pretty normal life before being sent away to boarding school, and why all that changed. I tell them about the bullying, about hiding my sexuality, about trying to take my own life, and how all that got me to where I am now. That can resonate deeply with older kids. At one school, one kid gets told off for strangling another kid, while I'm in the middle of a talk, which is darkly ironic. But I've had kids talk openly about being bullied; kids admit that they've tried to take their own lives; kids who have come out as gay; I've had kids break down because what I've said has hit home; I've even had teachers leave the room.

Before I give a talk, I always say that anyone is free to leave, because I never know how it's going to affect people. You don't always know what's going on behind closed doors. I'm not honest for dramatic effect, that's just the best policy, there's no point in sugar-coating it. And if you're honest, people can see you're speaking from the heart. I talk to them about being chased through corridors and beaten shitless on my bed. I tell them about not being able to escape and waking up every day thinking that the only way out was to take my own life. I tell them about picking up that knife, taking it to my room and cutting at my wrists. Some people find it difficult to hear, especially if they can relate to it directly. It can open up a Pandora's Box of emotions. But it's not about making people feel bad or confronting things they don't want to, it's hopefully about gaining strength from my experiences and the fact I'm able to speak openly about them. We get a lot of messages from kids, but we're not allowed to reply to them from a safeguarding point of view. That's really frustrating, especially when it's a heart-felt: 'Thanks for coming to my school and standing up and saying what you said, because it's given me the strength to come out myself.'

Here and now I just want to say to those kids: 'You're welcome, be strong.'

. . . .

I've never really thought about whether my sexuality is down to nature or nurture. I'm not even sure it's a relevant question. Society is obsessed with putting a label on everyone, but I don't think it's helpful. I used to see myself as something different, because of what society taught me, but not anymore. Now I listen to me. I'm no different to anyone else walking down the street, just because I prefer men to women. But some people don't get that. And because they see the difference, that creates nervousness or fear. That's when people start asking why people are like they are. To me, it doesn't matter why you are how you are, it matters whether you are accepting of who you are, and whether you let it define you. I don't think I let my sexuality define me. I chose to run The 401 Challenge to raise money for Stonewall because I know what they do to make life better for the LGBTQ community. I didn't run it for Stonewall because 'I'm proud to be a gay man'. I'm proud to be a human being, being gay is just a part of who I am.

I get frustrated with society always wanting to put people into separate boxes – labelling is never about equality because it emphasises the differences in people. The way I see it, we all bleed and wipe our arses in the same way! Well, maybe not, but you know what I mean. So many kids are unable to accept that they're gay because they think it means they won't be accepted by certain groups. I understand why a lot of people find sanctuary in the LGBTQ community. But I prefer to look beyond that, partly because of the Challenge and the almost Zen-like state running puts me in. It makes you think about things in a different way. It's not that I'm rejecting the LGBTQ community by any means, it's just that I don't feel my sexuality is that relevant to the person I am. Some people might think that sounds like I'm ashamed of who I am. I'm really not, it's completely the opposite: these days I'm so comfortable with who I am that I feel I don't need to belong to any group that is defined by the sexuality of its members. Isn't that the definition of equality and how we want people to feel?

In my opinion, there's still this masculine fear of gayness in some sections of society. That's linked to another stereotype, that if you're gay you can't be masculine. That's a load of bullshit! I feel, from my experience, that sexuality is on a scale, and we're no longer living in a world of stereotypes where if you're a camp, flamboyant man, you're necessarily gay and if you're a butch, sporty woman, you're a lesbian. Although, obviously, it's perfectly fine if you are. Those perceptions aren't disappearing fast, but they are slowly fading. More and more masculine men and feminine women are finding the courage to come out as gay, and the lines are becoming blurred, which I think is the way it should be. That's making some people even more nervous and fearful, because they no longer know what's what. But how they react is completely up to them; it's becoming increasingly obvious that they're part of a dwindling group. There are still lots of kids going through what I went through, but I'm convinced, from what I have seen, that most kids nowadays couldn't give a shit about other people's sexuality. I believe that 30 or 40 years down the line, the fight for gay rights won't even be on the radar because the battle will be won – at least I hope it will.

. . . .

IN PRAISE OF BEN SMITH

BRISTOL EVENING POST, 20 OCTOBER 2015

'...He has taken on an extraordinary challenge. And he has not wavered. He is fast approaching his 50th consecutive run. We wish him continued, blister-free success...'

. . . .

DAYS 50–60: In Dover on day 51, I get the news that Mum has been diagnosed with a chronic form of blood cancer. I've just done nine and a half laps of the harbour in the pissing rain, seen the same ferry come back as I saw leave in the morning, and I'm on my way to get some massage therapy when Dad calls. I'm sat in a petrol station car park, it's cold and dark and rain is crashing against the windscreen. Everything has suddenly been put in perspective. I don't want to give up, but I'm ready to let it all go, because what's happening to Mum seems far more important. I'm all set to tell Dad: 'Cancel everything, I'll just run around Lincoln for the next 350 days.' But then Mum comes on the phone: 'If you give up, I'll kill you! Whatever happens to me, don't stop doing what you're doing.'

A few years ago, Mum fell down the stairs and needed surgery on her back, after which everything that could go wrong went wrong. She contracted an infection in hospital, and a lot of irreparable damage was done. Things were so bad, she even started to question whether it was all her fault. Actually, it was just shit luck. But the accident and the aftermath had a profound effect on her, in terms of her confidence, self-esteem and independence. I think the accident was the trigger for everything that's happened since. But she's still an absolute trooper, all she's ever worried about is the rest of the family. Being Mum, she's just gutted that she'll have to step back from the project. I know when Mum's being serious and when she's not, and when to listen and when not. And I don't want her to feel guilty on top of everything else. So Kyle steps up, takes over most of Mum's duties, and I carry on. There's never really any doubt, and every marathon I run from here on in will be for Mum.

But it takes a while for the darkness to lift. Running through Kent, I miss home, I miss my friends and I miss Kyle, who is doing his PhD in Bristol while working part-time as a pharmacy technician, like never before. I ache all over and some of the driving conditions are leaving me a bit frayed. Driving down to Cardiff from Swansea, I was up on two wheels in a gale, white-knuckling behind a lorry, shouting: 'I'm gonna die! I'm gonna die!' This was a three-tonne van, three metres high, six and a half metres long. I found myself filling it up with water for ballast and was permanently worried it would flip over, especially when I was tired and not thinking rationally. Battling with a van is not really what you want to be doing when you're tired and cranky and coming down with a cold. In Canterbury, on day 54, I drive all the way to Bristol, to do the

Bristol to Bath Marathon, head back to Portishead to pick the van up, before driving to Sittingbourne in Kent, which is a distance of 190 miles.

I'm not super-human, I'm just a normal person, and I'm absolutely shot, completely and utterly knackered. So I resolve to be a bit more honest in my Facebook videos, to tell it like it really is. There was a temptation to keep a lid on the lows, because we thought some people might say: 'Well, nobody asked you to run 401 marathons in 401 days.' But there's no point pretending everything's hunky-dory when it isn't, because that gives a false impression about my life, and the whole point of the Challenge is openness and honesty.

But I can't be completely honest about absolutely everything. Believe it or not, there are people who have pissed me off. Some days, I run with people I can't wait to get away from. Some people have an attitude and whinge about stuff. I'm pretty good at talking about myself, hence this book, but there are lots of people far better than me, believe me. And I've listened to them. For hours. I'll be running with them and they'll be chewing my ear off. And there are people who want to challenge me and don't really get what I'm trying to do. I always try to run with the slowest people in the group, which is good for me, and good in terms of the Challenge's strategy, but it also helps motivate them and means they don't feel left out, because I know how it feels to be struggling at the back. But you'll get people saying: 'Hurry up! How long is this going to take? Are we really having another break?!' I feel like punching them. Seriously, who do they think they are? But I can't exactly post on Facebook saying: 'Great day today, apart from some idiot I ran with...'

Day 53 in Whitstable is one of the most memorable of the Challenge so far and one of the most memorable of my life. We made the decision early on that we weren't going to apply for the male world record, which stood at 52 consecutive marathons, for reasons I'll explain later. But the longer this Challenge goes on, the more I realise it's not about milestones or records, it's about meeting new people, inspiring them to achieve things they never thought they'd achieve, helping them build their confidence and self-esteem. This Challenge has a mind of its own.

Today, fellow runner Shirley completes her first marathon, having only ever run two, maybe three miles before. She had no idea how far she was going to run when she turned up, and ends up sprinting the last hill. Being part of making memories with someone like that is really special, and things like that are happening almost every day. Shirley didn't have that much confidence, but if you give somebody the belief that they can do anything they want to, there's no stopping them. I don't have a magic wand but the 401 is starting to cast a bit of a spell. People have started calling me the Pied Piper, and I'm finding it embarrassing to be called inspirational, because I just want to be me, and I've only been out running.

I think the project is working because I'm just a normal bloke. It makes people think: 'If Ben can run 401 marathons, I can surely run *one*.' All you need is positivity, it really is that simple. Shirley is the 32nd person to set a new PB so far, and that's what it's all about. This Challenge has become so much more than I thought it would be. And I'm just so happy to be living as me. In Crawley on day 60, I'm able to announce that The 401 Challenge has been nominated for two awards. My initial reaction on hearing the news was: 'Really? Why? I haven't done anything yet.' Apparently, I have, and I'm humbled and quite confused. At the same time, it shows that people are standing up and shouting about the Challenge, and the message is starting to get out there. Kidscape is really getting behind me, sharing my tweets and Facebook posts, occasionally sending someone out to meet me on the course and tell me what an amazing job I'm doing for them. I'm interviewed by BBC South East, and discover that almost £11,000 has now been donated. On top of that, three ladies from the Saints and Sinners Running Club complete marathons for the first time, and Tolu, my project manager, pops up out of the blue and runs a new distance PB of 18km.

• • • • • • • • • •

OCTOBER 2015 IN NUMBERS
Marathons: **31**
Miles run: **830.1** (average per day: **26.8**)
Running time: **162:08.27** hours (average per day: **5:13.49**)
Number of people run with: **349**
Distance personal bests: **38**
First marathons/ultra-marathons: **22**
Pints of cider: **15**
Flat whites: **31**

• • • • • • • • • •

Tim Osbourne, ultra-runner: *When I heard about Ben, I thought: 'This guy is insane – I've got to run with him and find out more!' The first marathon I ran with him was on day 80 in Oxford, and when he told me his story, it was quite unsettling. But it also told me that he was doing it for all the right reasons. He involved everybody, regardless of ability, and to see the look on someone's face when they'd done their first 10k or half-marathon, and the whole group had stopped to applaud them, was wonderful. People would be* in tears because they genuinely couldn't believe what they'd just done. Ben was just such a likeable bloke, and so much fun. I ran 12 marathons with him during the Challenge, and whenever it was someone's birthday, we'd all stop on a street corner and start singing 'Happy Birthday'. People must have been walking past, thinking: 'Who on earth are this lot?'

Ben is a bit of a clown, naturally funny, which I think got him through a lot of dark days. I saw him when he was quite down in the dumps, and I'd send him the odd text message or donate a tank of petrol to pick him up a bit. But he'd sometimes say to me: 'However down I feel today, it's not as bad as when I was being bullied in my former life.' I could relate to that healing side of running. I run a business, supplying and fitting kitchens, and sometimes it's overwhelming. It's long hours and my job doesn't finish when I get home. But when I'm stressed, I go for a run. Like Ben, running is my release, when I can forget about everything and the world really does feel like a better place.

I do ultra-running, where I'm out on the road for over 10 hours, and I'll sometimes end up in an almost hallucinogenic state. I remember Ben turning around to me during the Challenge and saying: 'Running that many miles in one go? That's mad!' To do what I do, you have to be mentally strong – but not 401 marathons in 401 days strong, that's completely off the scale. What a guy he is, and I'm proud to call him a friend.

· · · · · · · · · ·

ANTI-BULLYING CAMPAIGNER SET TO TAKE ON 77th CONSECUTIVE MARATHON IN STROUD

STROUD NEWS AND JOURNAL, 11 NOVEMBER 2015

'...The bullying I had faced at school had stripped me of my ability to accept who I was, but this is no more...'

· · · · · · · · · ·

DAYS 61–83: The weather turns harsh at the beginning of November and I'm beginning to wilt again before a special meeting with a very special woman. I first heard about Mandy when I ran in Bognor Regis with the Tone Zone Runners on day 45. Mandy was training for her first half-Ironman triathlon when she came off her bike and severed her spine in 2015. She was a fit, active woman and she ended up paralysed. Since hearing about her, I've wanted to meet her, because she sounds like such an incredible woman. I'm not disappointed.

I meet Mandy at Stoke Mandeville Stadium on day 83, and she does her first 5k in a wheelchair with me, around the track. Vicky Burr takes a great picture of the two of us, and just looking at it fills me with awe. I've never met a woman who is *so* positive, which is remarkable given the amount of shit she's been through. I find inspiration in her strength and she feels like a kindred spirit. I didn't go through the physical pain that Mandy went through, but I can empathise with the mental side of things, because we both came out fighting rather than giving up.

I have so many fond memories of the Challenge already, but it's very lonely at times, because nobody knows what it feels like. I've only met a handful of people who have got, 100 per cent, what I was trying to do, and Mandy is one of them. I hope everybody gets to meet someone like Mandy in their lives, somebody truly amazing. She truly is a breathtaking woman.

* * * * * * * * * *

Mandy Newton, Ben's heroine: *I was going downhill at about 50mph, lost control, hit a metal post and ended up in the middle of this bush. No one could see me from the road because the cars were going past too fast and too noisily. My phone had come out of my pocket (I had a banana, but that wasn't much use!). So I lay there for about an hour, thinking I was going to die, because I didn't think there was any way of getting help. And because I was still conscious, I thought God had struck me a pretty mean blow by letting me die so miserably. But I soon pulled myself together, and thought to myself: 'I'm not going to die, I've got four kids at home who need me. I'm going to get out of this mess.' Luckily, another cyclist came past, saw me in the bush, and called an ambulance.*

That night, I posted a selfie on Facebook, with a big smile and a message that read: 'Silly old Mandy, she had a little accident, hit a post at 50mph and broke 11 bones. I'm never going to walk again but I'll race you in a pink wheelchair!' All I could see was the fact I hadn't died. Sod the legs, you don't need legs to live a good life!

It was tragic for my family, and my husband and kids were sobbing in the hospital. But I kept on saying: 'Look guys, stop!

I'm alive, for God's sake! And I'm still your mum!' I don't like people being unhappy, sad or cross, so I just wanted everyone to see I was really happy to be alive. Almost every day, the nurses warned me I was going to crash mentally. But the crash hasn't happened yet. I have the occasional wobble. But when I'm having a few tears in the shower, I think: 'I'm actually bloody lucky that I'm able to have a wobble in the shower, on my own, where nobody can see it.'

My life couldn't be fuller and happier. I do scuba diving, water skiing, skydiving, hand biking. I'm doing the London Marathon, I want to go to Egypt this year, and I'm hoping to climb Mount Kilimanjaro. I give talks in schools about the challenges people face. Because we all have challenges in our lives, we mustn't be frightened of them. Challenges are good, because they help us to learn and grow. On one visit, there was a little boy with spina bifida, and when he wheeled into the classroom and saw me, his face was a picture. You could see him thinking: 'Oh, somebody on my wavelength.'

After I'd done my talk, another little boy, who must have been eight or nine, said: 'So, what do you prefer, your life when your legs worked or your life now?' I looked at this little boy in the wheelchair and thought: 'He'll never know what it's like to have legs.' And I told the truth: I said I would not change my life for the world, that I have had more fun in my wheelchair than I ever did before. All the able-bodied children were like: 'Really? Oh my God...' And you could see the little lad in the wheelchair's chest puff out like a peacock.

My perspective on life has changed. When I was in Stoke Mandeville Hospital, there was a 21-year-old girl in the opposite bed who couldn't even use her arms. She couldn't give or receive a hug, couldn't even feed herself. Quite often, if I was feeling a bit sorry for myself, I'd ask if I could help her, give her a drink or something to eat. I've always loved wrapping my hands around a cup of hot chocolate or ginger and lemon tea. But now when I do it, I think: 'That girl can't even experience this.' The really little things mean a lot more to me now, I suppose because the challenges have become a lot bigger.

When I met Ben, we did a lap of the track and he said to everyone else: 'No, I want it to be just me and Mandy.' He has this way about him of making you feel very special. It was very humbling, given what he was doing, that he seemed so in awe of me. I was thinking: 'For God's sake, I haven't done anything! You're the one doing 401 marathons in 401 days, not me, mate!' The following evening, he came back in again with Kyle. They'd had the pictures Vicky had taken framed. On one of them, he'd written: 'Amanda, you inspire me' – that was just lovely.

When you have a spinal injury, you can't control your wind, so I kept blowing off because we were laughing so much. I couldn't help it! But I kept thinking: 'I've never even met this guy before and I'm sitting here, blowing off!' He was like: 'Hey mate, don't worry about it. You don't have to stand on ceremony for me.' He just had that way about him: it didn't matter who you were or what you did, he just made you feel at home and very relaxed. He's not full of himself, he really didn't seem to think that what he was doing was a massive thing. That's why he had such a massive impact on me, and I think that's the appeal for a lot of people. Because he's just a normal guy, he makes other people believe they can do anything they want to do.

CHAPTER 8

His Saving Grace

It's important that people know that the creation of The 401 Challenge was a gradual, organic process – there was no lightbulb moment, and there doesn't have to be one, you just have to open yourself up to opportunities. I'd learnt to run, was doing all these marathons all over the world and loving the adventure, while figuring out that I didn't want much to do with my old life. I knew I wanted to do something that had never been done before, for causes important to me, but it involved a lot of trial and error: 'Maybe I could do this? Maybe I could do that? Oh. My. God. What if I did this? Let's see where this takes me…' I changed my way of thinking, stopped saying no and focused on what made me happy: The 401 Challenge was the result.

When I looked up the male Guinness World Record for the most consecutive marathons, it was 52. I thought: 'That doesn't actually seem like much.' It sounds mad written down like that, but that was my mindset at the time, because running had got me thinking that anything was possible. I'd done 16 marathons at that point – although not one after another, day after day – and was signed up to a further 14. I was running all over the world, having some crazy adventures, loving life, so trying to break the world record just seemed like the natural next step. But when I looked at the criteria, there were all these rules, one of which was that you had to run an official marathon every day. I emailed the Guinness World Records team and said:

'What do you mean by an "official" marathon?'
'We mean an official marathon. It needs to be timed and measured and ratified by an official body.'
'But you do know there isn't an official marathon every day?'
'Yeah, but that's part of the challenge.'

It was madness, they effectively expected you to set up your own event every day, sell tickets, promote it, and everything else that goes with organising a marathon. I assumed that was why the official world record was 'only' 52, and why it was held by a Japanese guy who ran around a track every day. So that ruled that out. I wanted to raise awareness, and how enthralled would people be by some bloke running around a track? And how bored would *I* be? It must have sent that poor Japanese guy loopy, and it was just so restrictive, which didn't sit well with what we were trying to do. So I made the decision to ignore the world record. Anyway, it actually turned out that a few others had done a lot more than 52, unofficially. A Belgian guy, Stefaan Engels, had done 365 in as many days in 2010–2011, and an Australian couple, Alan Murray and Janette Murray-Wakelin, had done 365 in as many days in 2013, before running a 366th on 1 January 2014. There was also a Spanish guy, Ricardo Abad, who had run 607 consecutive marathons, between 2010 and 2012, and some monk had allegedly done 1000, but we couldn't verify either of them. So I came up with a figure of 400, because I like round numbers. In hindsight, that's a ridiculous reason to add on 34 marathons, but that's the way my brain works!

But then, in April 2015, I went to America and did seven marathons in seven days across seven states, from St Louis down to New Orleans, as a kind of trial run, to see if my body would stand up to it. While I was there, I met an amazing guy called Larry Macon, who is in his

70s and has completed almost 2000 marathons, possibly more by now. When I told him my plan, he gave me lots of advice and made a suggestion: 'Why don't you have a victory lap?' Initially, I recoiled at the idea, because the British side of me thought it sounded all a bit American. But the more I thought about it, the more it made sense. I do like even numbers, but when I looked at the number 401, it just felt right. And I liked the idea of celebrating the success, putting it all together into one final event, bringing everybody together who'd organised the whole thing and run with me for the previous 400 days. The problem was, Tolu had already started organising all the branding, and when I got back to the UK, I said to her: 'Right, we're going to have to change everything – it's now going to be called The 401 Challenge.' She nearly killed me! But she soon got over it, worked her magic, and The 401 Challenge was born.

* * * * * * * * * *

Beverley Smith, Ben's mum: *I remember we were down visiting once, and Ben looked very stressed when we arrived. He went out for a run and when he came back, he looked fantastic: running was his saving grace. Once his marriage was over and he'd accepted in his head that he was gay, he began to live the life he wanted to live, which included running the world. That was his liberation. He let his mind go free and rediscovered his self-belief. All his life people had trodden on his self-belief. As a result, he'd trodden on any dreams he might have had.*

When he first came up with the idea for the 401, he looked at me and said: 'Do you think I can do it, Mum?' I said: 'Do you think you can do it, Ben?' And he said yes. So I said: 'Well, then you'll do it. When you put your mind to something, you always see it through. There will never be another day that is harder than the days you've had already in your life.' If we had poured cold water on the idea, he would have gone out and done it anyway. From a therapeutic standpoint, it was best to just enter his reality, however mad people thought that reality was. I'd just had a settlement for an accident, so we were able to buy him a decent van. As a mother, I just wanted to make sure he had food and somewhere warm to sleep. And I said: 'Even if I die, you can have a day off to come to the funeral, but that's it.'

Pete Smith, Ben's dad: *The first I knew he was planning anything was when I was in the flat he'd just moved into, helping him build some furniture. It was when he was having his Beautiful Mind moment and all his walls were wallpapered – top to bottom, wall to wall, not a word of a lie – with scribbled notes and graphs and drawings. Mind mapping, I'd call it. In the middle of all this was written: 'Do some form of big challenge'. And I knew that would have something to do with running. Before he found running, he'd had to play-act, conform with how the world wanted him to be: go to university, get an office job, earn good money, get married. Like a machine, an automaton. It surprised me, because he'd grown up in a military family, which is the opposite of all that, although I didn't know he was hiding this secret. It was the running club which helped him build his self-belief, because they never looked at him as anything other than a bloke who's turned up and wants to go for a run like them. Nobody was judging him and it was maybe the first time he'd been accepted by an open group or club. And running itself just flicked a switch in him. After his first half-marathon, he said: 'I will never do that again.' A few* days later, he registered for the Brighton Marathon. He realised he didn't have to be brilliant at it, as long as he enjoyed it.

He'd mentioned cycling across America before, but I wasn't that convinced because of the logistics involved. But even then, I said: 'Fantastic, crack on.' You've got to support your children, full on, from day one. It might sound callous, but if it's not going to work, it's up to them to find that out, it's not your place to tell them. He soon worked out for himself that he wasn't going to be able to do it. But one day he said: 'I've decided I want to try to run 401 marathons in 401 days.' And I replied: 'Fine.' After that, we got straight down to planning. He had most of it already worked out in his head. He'd already decided he'd be running around England, Wales and Scotland, but not Northern Ireland, purely for logistical reasons. He'd planned a rough route in his head, so that he'd be in the South for certain official marathons, and not in Scotland for winter. He put a huge amount of time and effort into it. And because he looked so determined, I thought: 'Yeah, he'll probably get there.'

He then spent the next 18 months working out if his body was capable of doing it, by running all those marathons. He ran in different climates, different weather, and when he ran seven marathons in seven states in America, I knew his body was quite capable and his health wouldn't be an issue. I was also confident of making it work logistically. The only thing I wasn't sure about was what was in his head. But I was with him in Germany for the 2014 Berlin Marathon, and after he finished, I looked at him and thought: 'Yeah, you've got it mentally. It will be money or injury that stops him from completing it, nothing else.' Once you've got it mentally, it

*takes a lot to stop you doing anything. Occasionally he would
say: 'Are you sure I should do as many as 401?' And I'd say:
'You don't want to stop at 70 or 100 or 200 and think: 'You
know what, I wish I'd done 401.' Millions of people have
done that, set themselves a target, reached it and thought:
'I wish I'd done more.'*

* * * * * * * * * *

It was so nice to be with Dad in Berlin, where he had spent time with
the RAF. He showed me the sights, we chatted and I asked his advice,
because I wanted to know how he felt about The 401 Challenge. He
had never been involved in this part of my life, but having this chance
to talk through the 401 plan with me, and seeing how comfortable
I looked after the marathon (I did it in 3 hours, 32 minutes, which
was my personal best until Oslo two weeks later, where I ran 3 hours,
17 minutes) convinced him I could do it. Having examined me up
close, he deciphered this huge change in me, and that I was now a far
stronger person.

Mum and Dad have never said: 'You can't do that.' It's always been:
'Whatever you want to do, we'll support you – what do you need from
us?' At the same time, they never dictated to me what I should do
with my life. Dad saw difficult things being done all the time with his
job, and made the seemingly impossible happen. I like the fact they've
given me the ability to do the outlandish, and never questioned it.
It's not that they didn't care about my health or my safety, they just
saw how important it was to me. Most people stick to the main road,
but I like to think I'm one of the people who doesn't think like that
anymore. I believe that, while maybe there is a plan laid out for you,
the fun part is doing everything you can to fuck that plan up. That's
when life gets interesting.

I had allowed a couple of weeks before setting off on the Challenge to try and put some weight on, and cut back on the running. I'd run 30 marathons in just over two years, 10 already in 2015, so didn't want to blow up before I'd even started. I moved out of my flat a week before the start of the Challenge and was still selling my stuff the day before – on eBay and a local Portishead website – because I didn't want to get fined for leaving it behind. In the end, I was saying to friends: 'Do you want any free furniture? Come and get it now, because I'm taking it to the tip, first thing in the morning!'

And, suddenly, there I was, standing on the start line in Bristol. That's life, things happen to you, you make choices based on those experiences, and sometimes those choices take you to a place you never dreamt you'd be, even a couple of years earlier. Those choices might be right or wrong, but they're usually right at the time you make them. And this is the choice I'd made now. This is what I wanted to do, so I did it. To be honest, I had no idea if running 401 marathons in 401 days was possible, but I was going to give it a bloody good go.

· · · · · · · · · ·

DAYS 84–91: During Anti-Bullying Week in November 2015, we launch The 401 Virtual Challenge, which was developed by a company called EtchRock, in conjunction with Virgin Money Giving. It allows people to join in wherever they are in the world – by running a 5k, 10k, half-marathon or marathon – to raise money for the 401, the aim being they'll run 401,000 miles between them. It's very cool, but I have to admit, I've been feeling down again. The weather in Essex is pretty bad, and the whole thing is becoming routine, which was never the intention. Out with the Harlow Running Club on day 85, I meet a little French bulldog wearing Chanel perfume, proof indeed that even dogs smell better than me. Every day as winter approaches there seems to be a new storm with a new name beginning with a new letter of the alphabet, and I've lost my wallet, although I don't know where or when. I hardly have a minute to speak to any of my friends, and I just want to be out having a few beers and a few laughs. Instead, I'm sat in a van, watching yet another episode of *Grey's Anatomy* on my laptop, as rain hammers on the roof. My head hurts, my body aches, I don't particularly want to be here…

. . . .

Annette Rainbow, masseuse: *I massaged Ben after marathon 80 in Oxford, having seen an advert on Facebook. If anyone is doing something extreme – swimming the English Channel, spending 30 days on a rowing machine – I like to offer help, especially if it's for charity. Bless him, Ben was just so tired and so tight. I felt like I could break him. He felt hard but very brittle, so that I almost didn't want to touch him. He was struggling to eat enough calories, was up late every night doing his social media, and he was definitely struggling trying to find any sort of rhythm. After Oxford, I followed him every day on Facebook, to make sure he was OK. But I thought he'd do it, because failure just wasn't part of his make-up.*

When I first met him, he hugged me, brought me a cup of tea and we sat and chatted. He thanked me for being so supportive and wanted to know all about me. That's Ben all over. I was bullied as a child, and it was really nice to speak to somebody who wanted to make a difference. I had so much therapy to deal with it all, and I feel like I'm through the other side. I'm also a hypnotherapist, and I've done my own research into why children bully. And Ben's honesty resonated with me. A bully's biggest weapon is their secret, and by Ben talking about his own experiences – saying it's OK to speak about what happened – he helps bring other bullies' secrets out into the open.

Ben is surrounded by people who are 100 per cent nice, and because of that, everything is possible. I'm now known locally as 'the lady who massaged the man from 401'. I talked a lot about Ben at work, put up posters, and I reckon between 10–20 per cent of my clients have taken up walking or running as a result of me meeting him. Some of them have even given up smoking. The Ben effect is huge. He's a role model, and has made an impact on so many people.

· · · · · · · · · ·

NOVEMBER 2015 IN NUMBERS
Marathons: **30**
Miles run: **791.1** (average per day: **26.4**)
Running time: **162:08.27** hours (average per day: **5:13.49**)
Number of people run with: **349**
Distance personal bests: **38**
First marathons/ultra-marathons: **22**
Pints of cider: **16**
Flat whites: **30**

· · · · · · · · · ·

DAYS 92–99: I'm surprised at how much we've struggled to get people to donate. Maybe it's because they still don't believe I'll finish, or maybe what used to be considered slightly unhinged has become the new normal. I should have made it 501 marathons instead. I get a nice boost in Norwich on day 92, when two old ladies who've seen me on the local news give me £15. I also seem to have picked up a bit of a Norfolk accent, and I've only been here a few days. That's one of the problems of being a military kid, accents stick fast.

People have started commenting on my diet on Facebook, because it's become a bit samey. My friend Jo keeps sending me text messages saying: 'Eat more greens!' For my favourite meal, I get a mixing bowl, rip up a whole cooked supermarket chicken – skin and everything – and chuck it in, pour in a pot of feta, a pot of olives, olive oil and coriander, add salt and pepper, add some microwaved Uncle Ben's rice, and eat the whole lot in one go, straight from the bowl, with the first thing that comes to hand. The naysayers don't know what they're talking about, it doesn't get much better. The weird thing is, my weight having stabilised, it's now starting to fall again.

On day 95 in Cambridge, I'm joined by my friend Nick, but no one from the local club has turned up to help us around the route. That's happened a few times: whoever we were dealing with has just given us a route and maybe not told anyone else from their running club. I first met Nick in Wokingham on day 63, and he ran with me for five days, heading towards Wales. When he first suggested spending almost a week with me, I thought: 'Oh shit, what if we don't get on?' It's like when you're on holiday and you're wary of speaking to anybody, in case they latch onto you and you can't get rid of them. But me and Nick are kindred spirits.

Nick works for the Metropolitan Police and his running has been a sanctuary for him, like it is for me. We both have a penchant for drinking cider in pubs, so we end up doing a lot of that on our travels. Put us together and we're like two little kids, always getting into trouble. I love Nick to death, he's probably the closest thing I've got to a best mate. In fact, he's like a brother, so when he finds out nobody from the local club turned up, he's really pissed off and I have to try and calm him down: 'For fuck's sake, why? Don't they know what's going on here?!'

· · · · · · · · · ·

Nick Dransfield, Ben's running brother: *I was out running and listening to the Marathon Talk podcast when they started talking about this 401 Challenge. When I got home, I said to my wife: 'There's this lunatic attempting to run 401 marathons in 401 days. He'll never do it.' I thought the bloke was crackers, but when I found out he was passing through Wokingham and had nobody to run with, I thought I'd best go and see who he is and what he's all about, before he breaks and falls to bits.*

I think Ben was a bit shocked when I rocked up and told him I was thinking of running with him for four days. But I thought: 'If we don't get on, I'll just cry off after one.' Halfway through that first marathon, he said: 'Right, I've got to stop for lunch…' Having run a few marathons myself, I said: 'I beg your pardon? What do you mean, stop for lunch?' We went into a pub in Wokingham and Ben started eyeing up the cider list. And I was like, 'You can't have lunch and a cider at half-time in a marathon!' I forced some food into me but it just didn't sit well. By day four, I was totally on board with the whole ethos – 'Right, where's the next pub? Let's have a nice bite and crack on with the second half…' When I realised it was simply about doing the distance and not trying to break any records, I thought: 'Actually, if he stays injury-free, this guy could do it.'

A few mates started giving me a bit of grief, saying, 'You're not even doing 1 per cent of what he's doing', so I thought I'd up it to five marathons on the bounce. We were both very childish, had a really good laugh on the runs and made a very good bond, so much so that we were soon calling each other 'brother from another mother'! He told me a lot about his life, and I shared my stories with him, because he's a great listener. I was shocked when he told me about his younger years, it was horrible to hear. Like Ben, I'm from a military background and went to boarding school, but was never bullied. But I saw bullying and, stupidly, didn't do anything to stop it. As a teenager you just want to be liked, so I was one of those kids who just stood there laughing along, which made me just as bad as the people who were carrying it out.

After the first day, I could sit back and watch how he dealt with it all. I got to see him in the morning, when it was just the two of us having a coffee or breakfast, and he'd be shattered, telling me how tired he was. If I'm shattered, I don't want to be friendly with people and posing for selfies but he had this game face that he was able to snap into, and suddenly any negativity would be gone. He'd be so welcoming and supportive towards people of any ability. If you had said to me two years ago that a marathon could consist of lunch, a pint of cider and mucking around for six hours, I probably would have said: 'Nah, that's not a marathon.' Now, having done it, I can say: 'It absolutely is.' If it says 26.2 miles on your watch at the end of your day, you've done a marathon.

The first day in Cambridge was another long one. It was on a Saturday, in an area with big running communities, so it was disappointing that nobody else turned up. I just thought: 'I don't expect everyone to go out of the way to run with him, but it

*doesn't take much to rock up and do 10km.' It made me sad –
not so much that he could have been on his own, more so that
people missed out on running with this amazing chap. Ben was
going through a rough patch – he had been on the road for
almost 100 days, away from his partner and family, and it was
taking its toll. But I never got the feeling he was wavering or
might quit. That's just not in his make-up and he was so focused
on the project. He just needed a shoulder: 'Come on, mate,
let's get through this and move on to the next one...'*

* * * * * * * * * * *

DAY 100: I celebrate passing 100 marathons with the Northampton
Road Runners, lots of cake and three personal bests. There is also a
mention from Chris Evans, who is a keen runner, on his BBC Radio 2
show, which is a very nice touch indeed and really makes my morning.

I make sure I'm running in the Lincolnshire area in the run-up to
Christmas, to be with my family, and in Sleaford, on 22 December,
I run with a really impressive kid called Jordan, who is only 16. He's
been bullied at school, for being a bit different, and he actually says to
me while we're running: 'I'm not sure I should do the whole course,
people might think I'm weird.' So I tell him: 'It's completely up to you
if you want to do it or not, but I promise you, once you've done it, you
will get nothing but positive feedback.' His mum is following in the
car, keeping an eye on him, making sure he's hydrated, and he ends
up running his first marathon. That just blows my mind. That night, I
post about him on social media, and he gets thousands of messages of
support from the running community. Three days later, on Christmas
Day, he runs his second marathon with me!

* * * * * * * * * * *

RUNNER TO COMPLETE 100th MARATHON IN NORTHAMPTON

NORTHAMPTON CHRONICLE AND ECHO, 9 DECEMBER 2015

'...The 401 Challenge isn't about being a victim, it is about showing people that no matter what you go through growing up, there can always be a positive outcome if you want there to be...'

· · · · · · · · · ·

DAYS 116–122: Christmas Day is actually quite normal, apart from the marathon in the morning. And the fact I get to eat two Christmas dinners. Funnily enough, I get a lot of running kit as presents, most of it waterproof gear. Better late than never! It's nice to be at home in Lincoln, but I'm constantly thinking about having to leave again, which doesn't make it the most relaxing Christmas Day.

The turnout in Nottingham on day 120 is the biggest of the Challenge so far, with 54 people running with me, but on New Year's Eve, day 122, Derby blows Nottingham out of the water with 74 people, which, given the rivalry between the two cities, the Derby lot find highly amusing. Unfortunately, on the way round I accidentally turn my watch off, so when I get to the scheduled finish I have to run three more miles. It's funny how many people want to pick at the data, keyboard warriors on forums who just want to discredit you. It seems they don't really understand why or what I am doing, so I didn't want to give them any ammunition. With 122 marathons behind me, and 279 to go, I bid 2015 farewell.

· · · · · · · · · ·

DECEMBER 2015 IN NUMBERS
Marathons: **31**
Miles run: **818.6** (average per day: **26.4**)
Running time: **158:12.19** hours (average per day: **5:06.12**)
Number of people run with: **541**
Distance personal bests: **36**
First marathons/ultra-marathons: **19**
Pints of cider: **16**
Flat whites: **31**

CHAPTER 9

A State of Disbelief

If I'm being honest, not everybody gets what I'm trying to do or makes good on their promises. Certainly, 99 per cent of the people who have got involved – whether by offering me a bed for the night, feeding me, giving me massage therapy for free, turning up to runs with shopping bags full of food – are wonderful. The amount of Jaffa Cakes I've been given – because I once mentioned I liked them on Facebook – is ludicrous, my van's shower is full of them. I've even had to put a post out: 'Can't eat any more Jaffa Cakes…' But there have been people who said they'd help out and haven't, which makes me distrust people and means the core team have had to pick up the pieces. But I guess that's the same with anything, and you figure these things out as you go along.

The doubters I cut out quite early, like a cancer. It's not that I need to be surrounded by positivity all the time, but if you haven't got anything nice to say, don't say anything. There are social media trolls, people who are pretty nasty to us. One guy said he wanted to pour petrol on me and set me on fire. Who knows why, there are lots of sad weirdos out there. But it never really bothers me, and I've been lucky that the horrible stuff is very minimal, and only really happened right at the beginning. Negative comments on social media are deleted straightaway, and the comments section has even become self-policing – my supporters will jump on any negativity and stamp it out in a flash. I think the fact I'm running to highlight bullying helps keep it to a minimum.

A couple of running clubs have told me they don't want to get involved, because of one of the charities I'm raising money for. As they made clear in the email, it wasn't Kidscape they had a problem with, so it had to be Stonewall. People can see that sometimes my next port of call changes on the website and start asking why I'm not running there anymore. We never call them out on it, because they are entitled to their views. Also, we only spoke to one person at each club, and that person's views don't reflect the views of all the running club's members. So we always just say: 'Sorry we won't be running in your town as planned, due to logistical issues.' Draw your own conclusions! But what's great is I'm talking about literally a couple of running clubs in the entire country, so the project is proving that most people don't have any issues.

There are people keeping tabs on us in the running community, making sure I run what I'm supposed to be running, which is fair enough. I'm sharing my routes and distances on the website Strava, but my first watch broke, which means there are some gaps. I have the data, I just can't upload it, which is frustrating, because there were a few people on running forums trying to discredit me. Thankfully, others have jumped to my defence, confirming that they've run with me and uploading their own data to prove I ran the full distance. Then there are those who want to challenge me. On one course we end up lost in some woods, three miles from the end, in the pitch-dark, in the teeming rain, because somebody keeps changing the route. It's not that they want to get us lost, but I assume it's that person saying: 'Let's see what you've got.' We all end up running an ultra-marathon, and I'm so annoyed, but I don't show it. Afterwards, I shake the person's hand and say: 'Thanks for that, that was a really good course.' They haven't broken me, it takes a lot more than that...

* * * * * * * * *

Nick Dransfield, Ben's running brother: *There were a few people questioning the project on social media, asking if Ben was really doing a marathon every day. I liked to respond to these people: 'I've been out with him and I can tell you he is most certainly doing one every day.' Some members of a well-known American forum like to call out British runners for cheating, and in some cases they have been proved right. They questioned Ben a little bit, until they started looking at the stats and realised he was legit. He wasn't doing it quickly, there were no world records on the line, but he was doing his 26.2 miles every day. Hats off to anyone who covers 26.2 miles – however they do it, it's time on their feet.*

A few times we ran and people got the wrong end of the stick, sprinted off and started reeling off seven-minute miles. I was thinking: 'Come on, guys, this chap's done a few marathons and his legs are a bit sore. Wind it in a bit!' Some people just didn't get it, but the vast majority did. They found that it was more fun running at a slower pace because it meant that you could chat to people, have a laugh, take in the scenery. It was just more sociable and enjoyable. Ben repackaged things, so there are now people who never would have thought of doing a marathon who can say: 'Actually, I did that marathon with Ben. Maybe I'll enter London or New York, or wherever.' Ben showed them that 'normal' people can do a marathon. With a bit of hard work for a few months, you'll get round, no matter what size or shape you are, or what your running background is.

• • • • • • • • • •

DAYS 123–127: I sometimes get really cross when nobody shows up. I wonder if I should feel guilty about feeling like that because people have other commitments and the world wasn't suddenly revolving around me just because I'd decided to do this crazy Challenge. But then I think: 'No, actually, I've put a lot of effort in, and if people have said they want to get involved, stick to your word, don't let us down.' I've been leaving it to running clubs to get the word out, rather than social media, and it's always the individual who lets us down, and not the club itself. Some will give you absolutely everything – people to run with, a bed for the night, dinner and breakfast – others make a minimal effort and a few do nothing at all. Dad will sometimes have to map out routes himself, while sometimes we get sent pictures of routes to work out for ourselves.

Liverpool is an amazing city for running, and there are a lot of 401 supporters there, but when we arrive, only one person from the local area turns up. After we leave, we have a load of people contacting us and saying: 'When are you coming to Liverpool?' I reply: 'We were just there!' They say: 'Why didn't you let us know?' And I say: 'We did!' Suzie Mills from the Teignbridge Trotters is the only person who does turn up in Liverpool on day 127. Thank God she does! Back in Truro, on day 18, she told me her plan was to do her first marathon a year to the day from her first ever run, and this is her day of reckoning…

• • • • • • • • • •

Suzie Mills, Teignbridge Trotters: *That was an awesome day in Liverpool. It was just me and Ben, and it was just so nice having him to myself, sometimes chatting, sometimes running in silence. Before the start, he broke the day down for me: 10km, stop for coffee and cake, 10km, stop for lunch, 10km,* stop for coffee and cake… He broke it down into manageable chunks and didn't care how much time it would take. He just wanted me to feel like I'd accomplished something, proved I could do anything if I really focused on it. The first six miles went by quite quickly, the legs were warming up nicely, text messages were pouring in and there were no niggles. But after running along the Mersey and reaching the halfway point at the pier head, my feet were starting to hurt a bit and I was getting a blister. In training, I'd managed to get up to 16 miles, which left 10 miles that were very much unknown territory.

With seven miles to go, we sat down in Sefton Park and I read some of the messages of support on Facebook. My legs were heavy, the blister had multiplied, but I knew I was going to do it. Running along the Mersey for the second time was amazing. The sun was setting and I could see the lights of the Albert Dock getting closer with every step. I'll never forget the encouragement and support Ben gave me during those last few miles. He was literally running around me as I was trudging forward. He knew I was struggling, so he started saying: 'OK, we'll run to there and then walk to there.' He made it seem possible. It was like a metaphor for life: break it down into manageable chunks, don't think too far ahead, just take the next bit as it comes. Hobble to that next bit, then maybe you can carry on running from there. With about a quarter of a mile left, just before we reached the pier head again, Ben ran on ahead because he wanted to film me coming in. By that point I was more walking than running, but I was determined to run to the finish. I don't know where it came from, but I ran with everything I had left…

It was dark and it was raining, but I just felt elated that I'd done it. I think both of us expected tears, but for a while afterwards I was just in a state of disbelief. In the space of a year I'd gone from not running at all to running a marathon. I just couldn't grasp it. But that's what Ben did, made the seemingly impossible possible for people all over the country. On The 401 Challenge Facebook page, it seemed like the whole running community had got behind him, was willing him to carry on, willing the project to be a success. And you'd read about all these people doing PBs, and that inspired other people, who then wanted to run PBs, so there was this snowball effect.

. . . .

MAN TAKING ON 401 MARATHONS IN 401 DAYS RUNS THROUGH BOLTON

BOLTON NEWS, 25 JANUARY 2016

'...I never wake up saying I don't want to do it, but my confidence wavers. But once I am on the starting line, that's it, there is no stopping me...'

. . . .

DAYS 128–148: On day 129, a mass of runners from Warrington Running Club are waiting for me at the start, all wearing big smiles and opening their arms in support, and my previous two days are forgotten. Twenty of us end up recording a video in a guy called John's bathroom – random, I know, but that's The 401 Challenge for you.

Moving through Manchester, Stockport and into Macclesfield, the groups continue to grow and the warmth of the North continues to shine through the murky weather. My two days in Manchester see me run with the Chorlton Runners and camp out in the car park of a pub. In Stockport, we get our biggest group yet, almost 250 runners – it's like a controlled riot. On day 133, in Macclesfield, I get to run with another incredible group of people (146 of them, a massive new record, including Neil, the leader, who is an absolute gent and really gets what we are trying to achieve) and then it's time to make my way across the Pennines, something I'll find myself doing a lot – from east to west, west to east – over the next few weeks. When I arrive in Sheffield for day 135, the weather is turning and snow is forecast, which makes me worried about losing control of Florence in the icy conditions, damaging her and scuttling the Challenge.

On day 135, I'm joined by Ben, Jane and a few other members of the local club, including Helen, who only flew in from South Africa six hours earlier, and we run around Ladybower and Derwent Reservoirs, where the 617 Squadron practised for the Dambuster raids in World War II. On to Doncaster for days 137 and 138, then to Hull for days 139 and 140, where running on flat ground is a welcome relief. Next to Brough, Goole, Wakefield, Bolton, Wigan and Southport, before I reach Blackpool, where I run with kids from a local disability school and am forced to take shelter from the raging wind in the arcades, where we run among the slot machines. Also in Blackpool, I get to run with Kyle's mum for the first time, along with her friend Chez. Chez and Pat manage their first half-marathon distance that day, which is an incredible achievement considering they have only just taken up running.

· · · · · · · · · ·

EXTREME ATHLETE RUNS THROUGH SOUTH LAKELAND

THE WESTMORLAND GAZETTE, 16 FEBRUARY 2016

'...I've run something like 4,290 miles so far – if I could walk on water, that would be from here to the Afghanistan-Pakistan border...'

JANUARY 2016 IN NUMBERS
Marathons: **31**
Miles run: **823.5** (average per day: **26.6**)
Running time: **166:03.03** hours (average per day: **5:21.23**)
Number of people run with: **639**
Distance personal bests: **31**
First marathons/ultra-marathons: **24**
Pints of cider: **15**
Flat whites: **31**

DAYS 149–172: In Preston, on day 149, I find myself wading calf-deep through ice-cold water, while in Bradford, on day 151, I'm left for dead by pupils from Bradford Academy, who are just so fast! It's snowing again in Leeds, where a final, desperate plea from Dad results in about 30 people rocking up and fighting over themselves to plan the route when we next visit. In Selby, the wind picks up and it's unsafe to drive

▲ Me aged three, at home in Germany, waiting for Father Christmas.

▶ With fellow runners in the USA during my seven marathons in seven days challenge, in preparation for The 401 Challenge.

▼ Florence the campervan in all her glory!

◀ Caught in the middle of Marathon 210 – so happy that I found a cider stop!

▼ Marathon 341 in Pontefract – jumping for joy!

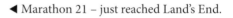

◀ Marathon 21 – just reached Land's End.

▼ Me, Kyle and Hiten Vora (Children In Need) at the Virgin London Marathon 2017. This was also Kyle's first ever marathon!

▲ The first 401 Festival of Running held on the August bank holiday weekend in 2017, to raise funds for The 401 Foundation.

◀ Marathon 355 – in Bangor, scared at the feat that lies before me!

▼ Me and Nick during the official Bournemouth Marathon in 2016 (Marathon 398). This was my fastest marathon in the Challenge (3 hours, 55 minutes). There was an amazing crowd and atmosphere.

◀ In Holyhead for Marathon 356, feeling like I'm on top of the world.

◄ With Chris Evans and Vassos Alexander after my interview on the Chris Evans Breakfast Show on BBC Radio 2, April 2016.

▼ Marathon 83 in High Wycombe – getting the calories in for breakfast!

► Kyle's mum and dad, Pat and Colin, at my final marathon. This was Pat's first marathon and Colin's 31st marathon.

▼ Marathon 82 in Aylesbury with Mandy Newton on her first 5k after her accident.

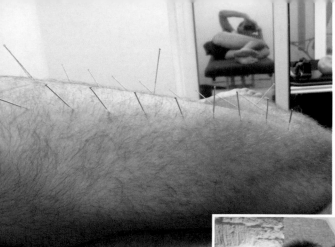

◀ Enduring a dry needling session at JamPhysio after Marathon 284, after temporarily pausing the Challenge – part of how physiotherapist Jamie Murphy restored me back to health in just five days.

▶ My mum and dad, Bev and Pete, at Dad's 60th birthday party.

▲ With Jamie from JamPhysio – this incredible man saved me and the Challenge!

▶ Enjoying a cryotherapy session, donated by the Chris Moody Centre, after Marathon 100 in Northampton.

▲ Running in Macclesfield with the brilliant Macclesfield Harriers.

◄ Half way through my 127th marathon, with Suzie Mills, who would go on to complete her first marathon in Liverpool exactly one year to the day she started running.

▼ Marathon 133 in Macclesfield with the amazing Macclesfield Harriers.

◄ Me and Baroness Tanni Grey-Thompson at the Worcester City Run, September 2017.

▶▼ At the very end of the challenge – the finish line of Marathon 401 in Millennium Square, Bristol.

▼ Kyle and I embrace after I complete my 401st marathon in 401 days.

▲ In the middle of a school visit after the Challenge at St. Johns Primary School, Hampshire.

◄ Talking to Steve Cram at the Virgin London Marathon Expo 2016 – the Virgin London Marathon in 2016 was my 237th marathon.

► 24/05/17 – after I proposed to Kyle. 5 months of planning paid off!

◄ Collecting the Helen Rollason Award from Paula Radcliffe and Tom Daley at the BBC Sports Personality of the Year awards, 2016.

the van, so we hitch a lift with the local fire service. In Bridlington, on day 155, the wind batters the hills, but the guys from the fire service keep me going. And on day 156, I run down the disused railway track from York to Selby, with soldiers from Catterick Garrison, wearing 15kg backpacks.

I make my way back across the Pennines via Wetherby, Harrogate, Keighley and Skipton, through Burnley and Lancaster, before heading up into Cumbria. The scenery and people around these parts are just incredible, but the routes are tough as the weather is getting bad again. In Carlisle, I meet the amazing DH Runners, who take me under their wing and I have a blast. We have such a good time, I decide to change the route, to ensure we run in Carlisle more often, and it becomes the third most-visited town in the Challenge.

After Carlisle, I make the trip back across the Pennines via Barnard Castle, Darlington and Richmond. In North Allerton on day 172, my partner Kyle, the man who hates running with all of his being, joins me for a few miles, which lifts me immensely. Then it's on to Thirsk and Scarborough, where I witness a miracle: a man drives past in his van, reverses back, winds down his window and says: 'I've seen you on the news, here's twenty quid.' I'm thinking: 'Twenty quid out of a Yorkshireman, that's the equivalent of a grand out of a southerner!' I can say that because both my parents are from Yorkshire...

But it's not just Kyle and his mum Pat who have joined me out on the road: Kyle's dad Colin ran his first marathon with me in Launceston on day 27, on his way to see his family in Truro, having left Preston at 4.30 a.m. He was wearing a pair of £10 trainers from Aldi and only planned to do five miles, but ended up doing the whole thing, and has done quite a few with me since. Colin is a lovely bloke, with a heart of gold, and he and his mate Pete like to run on either side of me, stopping people from talking to me if I'm going through a rough patch, as well as constantly taking the piss, all in good spirits. Colin's seen me at my worst, I've seen him at his worst, so we've formed quite a deep bond. That's the nature of the project: people have just got caught up in it, and it's certainly brought me and Kyle's family and friends closer together.

* * * * * * * * * *

Colin, Kyle's dad: *We went to a Northern Soul night, in the tunnels at Bristol Temple Meads, and Kyle brought Ben along. Kyle said: 'This is my boyfriend and he's going to attempt to run 401 marathons in 401 days.' I thought: 'Oh, right. Is he all there? Is something seriously wrong with him? Hasn't he got a job? Where's he going to get his money from?' And I said to Kyle: 'Well, you won't be doing any of it, will you?' I was in the Army, so had some idea of what it would take, both physically and mentally, so I was sceptical. But after I ran with him in Launceston, I thought: 'Hang on a minute, he's run nearly a month of marathons, this might actually happen.'*

I thought I'd come along and do maybe five miles, but there were a lot of people there that day and we all pulled each other along. I got to five miles and thought: 'I don't mind this pace, I'll do a bit more.' Then I got to 10 miles and thought: 'I've got this far, I might as well do half of it.' Then all of a sudden I've done 19 miles and I'm thinking: 'Ooh, this is starting to hurt a bit now, why didn't I go back earlier?' Ben asked me how I was holding up, and I remember saying: 'There's some woman running behind me, sticking knitting needles behind my knees, I'm gonna get her when we've finished...' I got to the end and Ben gave me a bollocking: 'You're never running with me again unless you get yourself a pair of proper trainers.' So the following weekend, I did.

I ran with him again in Birmingham and on Boxing Day in Lincoln, and I couldn't help noticing that while I was blowing out of my arse at the end of each day, he was bouncing all over the place. I'd be thinking: 'There's something seriously wrong with this lad. I know I'm giving him 25 years, but surely it must be hurting him a little bit?' But just coming up with an idea like that tells me that you're halfway there mentally. He basically picked the idea of running 401 marathons out of the air and convinced himself he could do it. And what a lot of people didn't realise was that he'd thought it through, come up with the idea of people running with him, even if it meant only running a mile, which must have helped immensely. And just the smile on those kids' faces when he visited them at school in the morning must have made running the next 26.2 miles that much easier. But he still had those long days, when he was on his own in the middle of nowhere and the weather was closing in, and he must have extraordinary mental strength to have got through that. And if anyone doubts Ben's powers of persuasion, all they have to do is look at my wife Pat. Before she met Ben, I'd never seen her run for anything…

Pat, Kyle's mum: When Kyle explained to me that Ben was going to run 401 marathons in 401 days, I was like, 'Yeah, right.' As you do. Even after he explained why he was doing it, it still didn't really compute. But on 1 September 2015, just before Ben was setting off, I thought: 'I might have a go at this running malarkey.' I got together with my friend Chez and went out for my first run, which was actually a mix of running *and walking. We knew he was running in Blackpool and Preston in January, so we thought we'd get up to 5k and do that with him. By Christmas, we'd actually got ourselves up to 10k, and when he came up to Blackpool, we both ended up doing a half-marathon. We were very broken, because that was our first time, but we had an amazing feeling of accomplishment.*

* * * * * * * * * *

DAYS 173–183: Kyle and I spend Valentine's night in a nice hotel, but running in Robin Hood's Bay, just south of Whitby on day 175, I feel slightly listless. I can't work out if it's Kyle's impending departure, a dodgy stomach or the fact I'm on my own with lots of time to think, which isn't always a good thing. I feel like I'm waning and, to be brutally honest, it just feels like the whole Challenge is starting to wear a bit thin. We're already making plans for the final day, 226 days away, and discussing setting up a foundation and business once I've packed the trainers away. It's a lot to take on and my mind is muddled. But I'm still looking forward to the next few weeks, back up in the North East. And right on cue, hundreds of schoolkids come out in Middlesbrough on day 177, some running alongside me, others lining the streets and cheering.

FEBRUARY 2016 IN NUMBERS
Marathons: **29**
Miles run: **768.5** (average per day: **26.5**)
Running time: **157:13.56** hours (average per day: **5:25.18**)
Number of people run with: **551**
Distance personal bests: **87**

First marathons/ultra-marathons: **40**
Pints of cider: **15**
Flat whites: **29**

In Sunderland, on day 183, it occurs to me that I've been on the road for six months non-stop. My beard is out of control, growing in several different directions at once, and my hair's a mess. I look almost feral. Kyle tells me I don't grow a beard like a 'normal' person, apparently it grows more like the gills you see on the raptors in *Jurassic Park*. What started out as a modest pile of dirty laundry in my van has grown almost mountainous and it's beginning to get a bit embarrassing, asking to use people's washing machines:

'Give it here, I'll do it.'
'No! It's alright, best I do it myself...'

Sunderland is where we meet lovely couple Steve Cram and Allison Curbishley, as well as Aly Dixon, who competed in the marathon for Great Britain at the 2016 Olympics. Steve is a massive Sunderland fan and gets us in the VIP box to watch a match, while Aly and the Sunderland Strollers get right behind the project. Linking up with Steve and Allison turns out to be a pivotal moment because without those two pulling a few strings, millions wouldn't have heard my story...

. . . .

Allison Curbishley, BBC broadcaster and former GB Olympian: *The secretary of the Sunderland Strollers forwarded me an email from Ben's 401 operations team, which was* *essentially his dad. It was quite a long email, explaining the Challenge and asking if any of the Strollers would like to organise a route and run with him. I rang Ben's dad, had a long chat, immediately fell in love with the project and really wanted to help. I said we'd add Steve's name to the event, to add a bit of regional stardust, rustle up some local media interest and contact some schools for Ben to drop in and talk to. And I hadn't even met Ben yet! But my hunch was right. As soon as I met him, I thought: 'I love this guy.' Within about 20 minutes, he'd told me all about Kyle, showed me pictures of him, and I felt like I'd known him for years. We joined him for a school visit, halfway through his run, and Steve ran the last six miles with him. Meanwhile, I'd spoken to a couple of people at the BBC, and Ben ended up talking to Chris Evans on Radio 2 and 5 Live, who just happened to be doing a show about bullying. We even managed to get him a free lunch at Frankie and Benny's – we told them about this mad idiot who was doing this Challenge and they put a spread on for him and about 10 of the Strollers. After that first day, it just snowballed into this great friendship.*

I assumed he was going for a Guinness World Record until he explained that they hadn't even applied. That told me he was doing it for all the right reasons. He wasn't doing this for Ben Smith to break records and become a legend, he was doing it purely to raise awareness about issues that were close to his heart and to help lots of people. It was clever how he got the clubs to buy into the project, challenging people to run personal bests with him and organise routes. But there were some days when it was literally just him. It's difficult to imagine what he was going through, getting up on day 320, or whatever day it was, and running a marathon in howling wind and rain. But the intimacy and immediacy of social media meant he was able to give people a taste of it, even if he was running in deepest, darkest Scotland, and the running community was able to get behind him and egg him on. So I was never really concerned about his mental strength because he seemed to be feeding off all that support and the people he was meeting every day.

Steve Cram, former 1500m world champion, 1500m and mile world record holder: *As soon as we met him, we realised what a great guy he was and what a great story he had. We just hit it off, we had a similar sense of humour and he was very self-deprecating. You sometimes meet people doing those types of challenges who are very locked into themselves, for obvious reasons. But Ben wasn't like that, he had all this energy and enthusiasm that he was able to spread to everybody around him. I found it remarkable that he was able to be so engaging when he'd already been on the road for so long and was constantly meeting people for the first time. I admired that so much because it was something I could never do. When I'm knackered and fed up, all I want to do is take myself off somewhere and grumble to myself.*

We spent that first day running with him and soon got what his ethos was. In Durham, a group called Mums on the Run presented him with this fantastic rainbow cake, the best cake I'd ever seen in my life – multi-layered and multi-coloured and everything. During my running career, I ate bacon sandwiches and cake and all sorts, so why not? There is a bit of snobbishness in the running community, and some traditionalists might turn their noses up at anyone who completes a marathon in five or six hours. But they're missing the point of what running has to offer people. We shouldn't denigrate anybody who wants to run: how long it takes is not the point and never has been. It's about getting off your sofa and having a go. We need that more traditional approach as well, because that's what produces elite athletes, but Ben is all about just getting people out running.

We helped Eddie Izzard in 2012, the first time he attempted to run 27 marathons in 27 days across South Africa. I remember trying to impress on him what it would take, in terms of preparation. When people embark on those types of challenges, I don't think any of them realise what they're letting themselves in for. The human body is incredibly resourceful and adapts very well, but if it does decide to break down, there's not much you can do about it, however positive your mindset. That happened to Eddie the first time around, when he had to stop after four marathons. But Ben retained this ability to not look too far ahead, not look beyond the day he was in, the marathon he was in, even the mile he was in. As an athlete, I trained hard every single day, twice a day, while elite marathon runners typically do 20 miles a day, 140 miles a week. But the idea of somebody getting up every day and running a marathon for 401 days, while still being able to give all this energy to everybody around them, was phenomenal to me.

* * * * * * * * * *

RUNNER TAKING ON MARATHON-A-DAY CHALLENGE REACHES SCOTLAND

GLASGOW EVENING TIMES, 11 MARCH 2016

'...I'm feeling tired, but I'm not going to complain...'

. . . .

DAYS 184–201: A mix-up means I'm on my own again in Northumberland on day 191, but this is where I have my magic moment on the beach – Holy Island stretched out in front of me, Bamburgh Castle to my left, sun directly above me, not a soul to share the view with, 5000 miles done! – and it makes for a nice bit of meditation. I think the locals feel bad about nobody turning up, because the following day, a member of Tweed Striders running club pipes me over the bridge into Scotland. I try not to cry, but it's *such* a beautiful moment.

Eight days later in Glasgow, I pass the halfway stage, and am party-poopered to within an inch of my life after finishing. Time to take stock: 201 marathons done, 200 marathons to go. On the minus side, I'm sick and tired of being wet and cold; on the plus side, I've now run with 3,300 people from something like 190 clubs. Over 350 people have run distance personal bests, about 140 of them marathons. We've also raised over £40,000, which is great, but still a whopping £210,000 short of the target. Even after 201 marathons, there are still people who don't think I'm serious and I still don't really know how the project is being perceived. There has been a lot of local media attention, but not a lot nationwide.

The lack of coverage is a little bit demoralising, but I understand it. The press likes to have a complete narrative to work with, and that wasn't going to be the case until marathon number 401, or unless something went wrong. And while the celebrations in Scotland are lovely, I'm very much aware I still have another 200 marathons to run, which is really quite scary.

• • • • • • • • • •

Trish Divine, one of Scotland's finest: *My husband and I are members of a Facebook group called Run for Your Life, so when we discovered Ben was heading to Scotland, I got in touch with the 401 team, which was actually his dad. Before we knew it, we were tasked with mapping out a marathon route for him.*

About a week before the run, Pete phoned and said Ben was a bit stuck for accommodation, so we ended up putting him up for a few nights. Sometimes you meet people who are special and it's hard to pinpoint why. I used to work in sales and often say to people: 'You only get a short amount of time to make a first impression.' And Ben made an enormous first impression in the shortest time. He just had that rare gift, he didn't even have to try. He was very open and exuded warmth. He had no airs and graces and put us at ease. He had this incredibly smiley face and was a chatterbox. I thought I talked a lot, but he was a different level! But it wasn't 'The Ben Show', he wasn't consumed by his own world, he was genuinely interested in us. Ben was getting organised in the bedroom when Jim walked through and said: 'I can tell that this is going to be a friendship for life…' It's worked out that way.

Jim Divine, another of Scotland's finest: *Both of us have been on the receiving end of bullying. We're a lot older than Ben, but Trish can vividly remember being bullied at school. It never took her to the brink of wanting to take her own life, but on her vulnerable days, dark shadows appear. But there's nothing like speaking to someone else who's been there. How does Ben trust and like people after what people did to him? That takes enormous strength.*

We did nine or 10 runs with him during the Challenge; hundreds of people turned up and everyone was in it together. It wasn't about being divisive or elitist, it was about the power of people doing something good together. Whoever turned up, it didn't matter how fast they were, how big they were, how old they were, they were included in this growing community. I think a lot of runners forget that at times. We all started somewhere, and all struggled with our running at some point. Ben didn't care if people were coming out to run for the very first time, he made them feel so welcome and made them realise that anything is possible if you put your mind to it.

The first time we ran, a guy at the start said: 'Right, I'm off to make tea and cakes for you.' We were like: 'What?!' We got about six or seven miles in, stopped at this guy's house and he had a big spread laid out for us – tea, cake, coffee and biscuits. Then, about an hour later, we stopped at a pub. Ben had bruschetta, burger and chips and a pint of cider, all on the house. People were gobsmacked. One of the guys was a regular marathon runner, and we looked at each other and said: 'I might be able to manage a bowl of soup…' But a few runs later, we were tucking into huge meals as well. That's definitely the way to do a marathon!

MARCH 2015 IN NUMBERS
Marathons: **31**
Miles run: **824** (average per day: **26.6**)
Running time: **160:57.29** hours (average per day: **5:11.32**)
Number of people run with: **477**
Distance personal bests: **61**
First marathons/ultra-marathons: **27**
Pints of cider: **16**
Flat whites: **31**

• • • • • • • • • •

MAN RUNNING 401 MARATHONS IN 401 DAYS RETURNS TO WARRINGTON

WARRINGTON GUARDIAN, 6 APRIL 2016

'...Ben Smith, 33, was supported by more than 100 runners, walkers and joggers along the route...'

• • • • • • • • • •

DAYS 202–238: I'm not in Scotland long this first time, as I have to get back down into England for the start of the official marathon season in April, starting with Manchester on day 223, which is the first time it really hits home how many people know about the Challenge. There are people cheering my name, asking for selfies and autographs, giving me high fives, fellow runners slapping me on the back and hugging me, many of whom I've already run with in other parts of the country, and I think: 'You know what? We might only have raised 40 grand so far, but we're beginning to have an impact and possibly change people's lives. Let's keep doing what we're doing.'

At the Brighton Marathon the following weekend, on days 230 and 231, BBC Sport comes and films me for a piece to be broadcast during the London Marathon, a week later.

People had been getting onto Eddie Izzard on Twitter, saying: 'Have you seen what this bloke is doing?' Brilliantly, *he* got on board and started tweeting about it. Others were getting a bit agitated that the BBC were ignoring me (which wasn't strictly true – some of the regional news programmes had been really supportive), but the BBC do their bit at the London Marathon to make the project explode. As well as the short film they show during the race, I'm given a wristband that says 'celebrity' (which amuses Kyle no end), plonked in a tent and interviewed by BBC Breakfast, Radio 2, Radio 4, 5 Live and various TV news programmes.

Gabby Logan interviews me on the start line, I'm chased down the Embankment by Colin Jackson and a camera follows me down The Mall on rails. I spot Kyle in the crowd, head straight for him and I'm shown on national television giving him the biggest kiss. Immediately I think: 'Well, if anybody didn't know before, they certainly do now...' I hug Tolu and Allison and the person next to Allison, who I suddenly realise is Paula Radcliffe. It's all so surreal and wonderful.

* * * * * * * * * *

Allison Curbishley: *After those first few days in the North East, we put Ben's team in contact with as many people as we could in other parts of the country. We knew Ben wasn't well-resourced or experienced in terms of media relations, but he* had such an inspirational story, we felt it was important that it was heard by as many people as possible. Nowadays, you have to do something really out there to interest the media, but I couldn't believe I hadn't heard about Ben before I did. Steve Cram told the BBC about Ben at a London Marathon planning meeting, and they hadn't heard about him either. So Steve just said: 'Look, it's a brilliant story, he's brilliant on camera, you've got to get him on.' That's when they sent a film crew down to Brighton and made this brilliant film. While Ben was running in London, I said to Kyle: 'As soon as they drop Ben's film into the coverage, when they've got 2.4m people watching, your donations will go through the roof.' I was stood with Kyle at the finish line when it happened, and everything went crazy – the donations, the social media, emails, texts, the lot.

He was just so lovable and articulate, without sounding self-pitying. He just seemed so genuine and was able to tell his story in a way that everyone could buy into it. Some of these big challenges I hear about seem a bit forced and it's all about the person rather than the cause. It might sound strange, but Ben rarely talks about himself – he talks about all the bad stuff he went through instead, which is almost like hearing him talk about another person. That's the thing I find most interesting about him, the fact he was able to flick a switch in his head, put all that rubbish behind him and change his life completely. And now, having done that, it's like the floodgates have opened. Suddenly he feels confident enough to share his story with everybody. He passionately wants to get rid of bullying, he passionately wants acceptance and equality for all people, and I just think it's

brave to speak out about that kind of stuff. That's the reason
he attained almost this cult following and The 401 Challenge
became like a family.

I love to talk and I love listening and I love a good story, and
most runners are the same. All most people want is an easy life
and a happy life, and when you see other people who have
made choices to make themselves happy and do good things
and give something back, you want to go on that journey
with them.

. . . .

The following morning, day 238, I'm meant to be running in Bromley, but I'm invited on Chris Evans' BBC Radio 2 breakfast show. So I'm up very early after a crazy night, jump on a Tube and am greeted outside Broadcasting House by a gang of running club members, all wanting to wish me good luck, which was very sweet. At the front desk, I tell them I'm here for the Chris Moyles show, I don't know why that name came into my mind, I knew who I was meeting – that's how tired my brain is. The receptionist looks at the security guard and they both raise their eyebrows as if to say: 'Who is this muppet?' Thankfully, Chris and his sports reporter Vassos [Alexander], who has written his own book about running [*Don't Stop Me Now*, Bloomsbury], are lovely. We see an immediate spike in donations and suddenly £250,000 actually seems achievable. But the glamour, if you can call it that, is short-lived. After my spot, I have to get a Tube across London, drive from Docklands to Bromley and run another marathon. Well, nobody asked me to do it…

APRIL 2016 IN NUMBERS

Marathons: **30**

Miles run: **796.9** (average per day: **26.6**)

Running time: **157:57.48** hours (average per day: **5:15.56**)

Number of people run with: **1050**

Distance personal bests: **98**

First marathons/ultra-marathons: **37**

Pints of cider: **15**

Flat whites: **30**

CHAPTER 10

Problems Staying Straight

DAYS 239–249: Milton Keynes Marathon in the can, I make my way up through Corby, visiting 19 schools in and around Grantham, in conjunction with Inspire+, a charity set up to provide quality PE and sport in schools. Spring has sprung, the weather is glorious and the kids are going ballistic. If even just one of those kids is inspired to do something they never thought they could, or gains strength from my story, it will have all been worth it. However, the next couple of days have been playing on my mind for a few weeks now, because it's time to return to my old school where so many of my demons came into being. I had been asked to give a talk to the whole school by the new headmaster. My old headmaster left a couple of years ago, but what I don't want to do is stand up in front of all those kids and say, 'It's not as bad now as when I was here', without knowing for sure.

So I arrange to meet with the new head and I say: 'I'm happy to come and do a talk, but hopefully you're fully aware of the problems I had here. So I need you to prove that you've got all the policies and procedures in place to combat bullying, and that they are being implemented.' The new head, who turns out to be a lovely man, gives me a heartfelt apology for everything that happened to me while I was a pupil at the school. More importantly, everything the headmaster said they did, they did – it wasn't just a pile of paperwork in the corner of an office, gathering dust, like it used to be. The school now has counsellors and student representatives from each year group and each house, making sure there is the necessary pastoral care. So while I'm nervous, standing in a chapel full of 400 kids, telling them about all the shit that happened to me while I was a pupil – the relentless bullying, the suicide attempt – it isn't particularly difficult, because now I have the confidence and determination I didn't have then, and I know the place has changed.

* * * * * * * * * *

Pete Smith, Ben's dad: *The school was now focused on the children, rather than profit-driven, and little touches showed how much things had changed. For example, the old headmaster used to have his office in a separate house, but the new headmaster had moved his office into the school, so he could see what was happening every day and the kids could pop in and see him if they had a problem.*

Ben will just stand in front of the audience, with no props or PowerPoint or any of those crutches that people use, and tell people his story. He had a good time that day; he pulled no punches, talked about his bullying and suicide attempt which can be quite harrowing for people to hear, and answered everybody's questions absolutely honestly. He told the kids he'd stood where they were now, advised them to use the system that was in place if they needed to, the system he himself wasn't lucky enough to have. I think he laid a lot of demons to rest that day.

Beverley Smith, Ben's mum: *One of Ben's old teachers rang me and said: 'I hear Ben is doing this wonderful Challenge, how fantastic! Would he consider coming to the school to talk to the pupils?' I wasn't sure about it, but I said we'd discuss it with Ben, and under no circumstances would he stay overnight.*

*We all turned out to support him, although he wouldn't let me
hear him talk, and still won't. He's happy for Pete to go, but it's
too raw and he knows it will upset me.*

*A number of sixth formers ran with him, including one
who ran the whole way. He was only going to run five or
six miles, but that's the type of person Ben is, he encourages
people to do their best.*

. . . .

YORK CHILDREN JOIN CHARITY RUNNER ON HIS 254th MARATHON

YORK PRESS, 11 MAY 2016

'…At Fishergate Primary School, in York, Ben told the children:
"It's really difficult to get up in the morning sometimes. But I
think about the reasons I'm doing this and that motivates me to
get out of bed…"'

. . . .

DAYS 250–284: Back up the North East coast and into Newcastle for
the second time, where I'm given tickets for United's game against
Spurs. Everyone seems in good spirits, despite the fact they've
already been relegated, and I'm introduced on the pitch at half-time
in front of about 50,000 football fans. I'm not sure anyone can hear
me, but I get a nice round of applause regardless. The following day –
day 259 – is my 34th birthday. I get involved in the launch of the
Durham 5 and 10k, where we meet up with Steve Cram and Allison

Curbishley again, and that night, I stay in a five-star spa hotel near Darlington, with Kyle, Mum and Dad and Tolu. Obviously, I don't look too smart, rocking up in sweaty running gear, but they don't seem to mind and let me park my van right out front. I don't have time for the massage they offered me, so Kyle has it instead – he had it good at times!

MAY 2016 IN NUMBERS
Marathons: **31**
Miles run: **824.5** (average per day: **26.6**)
Running time: **172:58.20** hours (average per day: **5:34.47**)
Number of people run with: **1118**
Distance personal bests: **127**
First marathons/ultra-marathons: **46**
Pints of cider: **16**
Flat whites: **31**

On from Whitley Bay to Alnwick, where I develop an umbilical hernia and end up in Alnwick Infirmary, which suggests that my body is beginning to rattle. On to Wooler, Northumberland, and then into Scotland for the second time. On day 264, the Jedburgh Joggers, a great mass of women runners, are out in force, and it's such a great day. But just before the Edinburgh Marathon on day 272, I start to get a niggle at the bottom of my back, like something I've never experienced before. At first, I explain it away as general wear and tear, because other parts of my body have hurt for three or four days before the pain has suddenly disappeared. That's the only way a body can survive doing something like this – if there's any form of negativity, you might as well give up and go home. Weirdly, I run a Challenge PB in Edinburgh, about three and a half hours, but feel terrible the next day.

I leave Edinburgh, run through Dunfermline, Kirkcaldy and up into St Andrews, where a gang of us recreate the famous slow-motion *Chariots of Fire* run on West Sands beach. But despite the smiles and larks on my Facebook video, my back is deteriorating. It's fine when I'm running, it's when I stop that's the problem, especially when I'm driving the van. Past Perth, Dundee, on to Arbroath, Montrose and Stonehaven, whose half-marathon route is notoriously hilly. And while I wouldn't say it's Stonehaven that finishes me off, it's certainly part of it. That night, my back completely seizes up.

I'm staying with friends, Carolyn and Geoff, in Inverurie, and they're having to ferry me in and out of Aberdeen on days 282, 283 and 284, because driving has become so painful. My back is starting to contort, almost concertina, so that I'm all bent over when I stand up. I know I have a problem staying straight, but this is taking the piss. On top of that, there is sciatic pain surging all over my legs. But even now, all I can think of is getting to day 300 in John o'Groats. It's fair to say I'm so focused on the Challenge that my perspective is completely shot. I dose up on codeine, stick my fingers in my ears and do my best to ignore the glaringly obvious, until Carolyn, the ex-nurse I'm staying with, gently insists I at least get my back looked at.

DAY 285: We ring the surgery and the doctor calls back and says: 'Can I just check it's 401 marathons you're doing? In 401 days? Right, let's try to see you in the morning...' I arrive at Aberdeen Royal Infirmary at the crack of dawn on the morning of day 285, and the lovely doctor takes one look at me and says: 'You need to stop.' I completely lose it and start crying. I'm tired, because I haven't been sleeping, and I don't want to hear this. Nothing else matters apart from achieving my goal and now someone is telling me it's over. I'm told that the problem is due to my umbilical hernia, which has caused my back to spasm, but they're not entirely sure. I want to carry on, but my team overrules me. At least I think they do – it's difficult to tell, because I'm off my face on painkillers. I don't think I'm shocked, and I might even be a little relieved – if I'm going to fail, and I do view it as failing, then at least it's for a medical reason and not because I quit.

After returning to Carolyn and Geoff's house on the morning of day 285, I post a forlorn video on Facebook, saying I have to take a break and that I feel I've let people down. It sounds irrational, but that's how I feel, because I've been so hell-bent on achieving this goal, and I've not raised £250,000 or run 401 marathons in 401 consecutive days, as I said I would. I tell my supporters and friends the plan is to be back on the road soon, but the truth is I don't even really know what's wrong with me. The video gets more than 300,000 views and people write some lovely messages, but I struggle to find the positives in any of them. I just want to go to bed, pull the sheets over my head and hibernate.

The decision is taken for me to get a train to Preston, where Kyle is now living, so I do. I'm just angry, because I feel like my body has let me down, and I wonder if I've done something wrong for it to do that to me. Some of the papers report that The 401 Challenge has broken down, and I heard that the BBC and ITV want to come and film me. I don't want to deal with any of this. Poor Dad and the media team (aka Kyle) are constantly battling, trying to control the flow of information. I've gone from concentrating on running to dealing with tiny little details, and my emotions are all over the place, ranging from despair to elation. I don't know how Kyle and Tolu put up with me over the next few days!

* * * * * * * * * *

MARATHON EFFORT ENDS

THE TIMES, 15 JUNE 2016

'...Ben Smith, 34, had completed 284 marathons since last year, running 7,440 miles across England, Wales and Scotland. But after a trip to A&E in Aberdeen at the weekend, he was forced to pull out...'

. . . .

I arrive at Preston train station having no clue how I got there, because of all the drugs, although it transpires I had to change twice. There's a massage therapist there called Brian, who knows Steve and Allison and has treated me before, but he tells me he doesn't know what's wrong and doesn't want to make it any worse. Luckily, he knows a man who might be able to get to the root of the problem.

Jamie Murphy has worked with Bolton Wanderers, Newcastle United, Manchester City and the New York Red Bulls and now has a practice called Jam Physio in Blackpool. He is an incredible man and not like any physio I've ever been to. In fact, I'd say his techniques are verging on wizardry. Jamie looks at me, gets me to do some exercises and stretches, and reckons he knows what's wrong. He sends me to have an MRI scan at a private clinic in Wilmslow and I'm diagnosed with something called spondylolisthesis, which is when a bone slips out of position at the bottom of the back. They also find a fracture in one of my vertebrae, a bulging disc, and all of this weakness has started to lock everything up, which was the body's way of telling me to stop. And because every little muscle in my body's core has locked up, it's got to the point where my spine has started to twist like a corkscrew and my nerves are being squeezed, which is responsible for the pain. Wonderful Jamie agrees to treat me for free and does so for almost 18 hours over the next 10 days. He describes the body as a padlock with a sequence so that when you get a pain somewhere, it's not necessarily where the problem is, because everything is connected. Sometimes you can have a pain in your foot because you've got an issue with your opposite shoulder.

Jamie is nicknamed 'The Butcher' for a reason: the things he can do with his thumbs are insane. He also does a lot of dry needling, which is similar to acupuncture, but 10 times more painful. In dry needling, the needles are kind of slammed in, and at one point I have 30 of them hanging out of me. I swear at Jamie a lot, and I'm not ashamed to say that I cry more than once. I have to keep reminding myself that he's just trying to find the sequence. Various other bones are put back where they should be, it's almost as if he's putting me back together. I'd done it with my mind before, so surely I could do it with my body? The BBC film me getting my therapy and, trust me, I didn't fake the pain. ITV Real Stories also come to interview me, but it all seems so pointless, as I just can't envisage getting back on the road, try as I might.

But seven days after breaking down, I'm able to run again. I have a conversation with Kyle and he seems supportive. The only other person who might be worried is Mum, but she knows what I'm like. Because of Jamie's background as a professional footballer, and the fact that professional sportspeople are constantly playing with injuries, he knows it isn't his job to tell me to throw the towel in. So he teaches me a new way of running instead, one that will better support my body. He works with me on exercises to activate my glutes – in layman's terms, to use my arse muscles more! – so that my hips aren't taking too much of the strain. It's not as easy as it sounds, but it's a more efficient way of running. And when you're taking almost 42,000 strides a day, you really need to be running as efficiently as possible. New technique learnt, although not yet mastered, I make the decision to carry on with the Challenge. Jamie is the saviour of the 401 and we'll always be indebted to him for that.

On Facebook, I announce that the revised plan is still to complete 401 marathons in 401 days, by tacking on a couple of extra miles every day. That way, we can still say I achieved what I set out to do. Nine days after I was told to stop, I pick up the van in Inverurie, drive to Inverness and book into a Premier Inn. I knock out three miles, to try out Jamie's new running method, before recording an upbeat video for Facebook. But all I can think is: 'Can I really do this?' From being something that seemed achievable, it now seems like an impossible mission.

* * * * * * * * * *

Jamie Murphy, wizard physio: *When Brian phoned me up and asked me to have a look at a friend of his, I said: 'Okay, no problem, but I'm fully booked for the next two weeks.' Brian said: 'You've got to see him quick. Please. He's doing this amazing thing for charity. Go on the internet, look up The 401 Challenge and phone me back.' I looked it up, phoned Brian back and said: 'Tell him to come in on Monday morning and I'll see him in between other patients, if he's happy to sit and wait.'*

Monday morning came around, and when I went into reception, I saw this guy wearing a blue beanie, all hunched over with his head down. Luckily, I got a cancellation, so I went back out and said: 'Oi, you must be the marathon man?' I'll never forget what happened next. He lifted his head up, and I saw he had this great big beard and these black, sunken eyes. I thought: 'Surely this can't be the guy?' He struggled out of his seat like an 80-year-old man and shuffled across reception, all stooped over and bent to one side, limping like a dog with a thorn in his foot. I thought: 'Wow. How has this guy done 284 marathons? He's got major, major problems...'

Apparently, a specialist in Scotland had told Ben that it was just a soft tissue problem. Within about two minutes, I knew it was far worse than that. His body was an S shape, and he couldn't move or sit up straight. It was quite evident that he had something protruding on the lumbar spine nerve, which was causing him to list to one side. I sat him down, asked him what he was on, and he replied: 'Tramadol, diazepam, co-codamol, a strong anti-inflammatory, and I'm taking paracetamol every couple of hours...'

Ben said he was worried the Challenge was over. I thought, 'Never mind the Challenge, you might never run again!' But I didn't tell him that. Instead, I said: 'Let's just see how you go.' During the consultation he poured his heart out to me, told me why he was doing the Challenge and how much it meant to him. He had a lovely aura about him, was such a likeable character, so I was sold – I couldn't let this guy down. I said: 'Right, I'll throw the kitchen sink at you and see what happens!'

He got two or three hours of treatment that first day, in between my regular patients, and I really put him through the mill. I pulled him and cracked him and stuck needles in places I can't even tell you. I went all the way down to his feet, popped bones back in that were out of place, all to get his muscoskeletal system engaged again. When I sent him away, I said: 'No more drugs!' That night, he posted a video, telling everyone the Challenge was back on track. I watched it and thought: 'Bloody hell, no pressure then...' I hoped I could put him back together, but not that quickly.

The following morning, he walked into the clinic with bright eyes and this big smile on his face. He said: 'I can't believe it, I feel so much better!' He was still bent over to one side, but there had been a massive improvement, which was down to his mental strength as much as anything I did. That week, I showed him how to work muscles that he'd never worked before, and he caught on very quickly. Soon, there was a part of me thinking: 'This guy could actually finish the Challenge.' I suggested we do a 5k in Lytham, to test things out, and you could see his confidence grow as he ran. We said our goodbyes, which was quite emotional, and two days later he did an ultra-marathon. For weeks afterwards, people were coming into my clinic and saying: 'Is he still doing it?' He was still doing it, but I was expecting a call at any time. It's very nice of him to say I saved the project, but we were just there to help him. It just shows that you can be in terrible pain and your body can be ready to break, but with drive and spirit, you can do almost anything.

. . . .

DAYS 286–296: I arrive at the sports centre in Inverness and BBC Scotland are waiting for me, and it's actually a nice distraction to be interviewed while running. We do part of the Loch Ness Marathon route, running almost to the sea and back along the river, before chasing the ferry along the towpath. My back hurts a bit, and so does my arse, but I end up running 30 miles, which is the most I've ever run in one go. I'm completely and utterly shocked, because I went into today thinking I was going to die. I go to sleep that night with a feeling of accomplishment, before waking up the next morning feeling like shit. I can't move and it's not just my back that hurts, it's everything. My confidence isn't what I thought it was, and all I can think is: 'Please don't let this be like the first 50 days all over again.' I manage to crawl out of bed and drag myself to Dingwall. Dingwall is beautiful and horrible at the same time. I whinge and moan and cry throughout the run, and even start thinking: 'If I gave up now, would that really be a bad thing? Most people would have chucked it in by now. Most people wouldn't have started. I've already done enough, surely?'

I have no massage therapy booked in, so Kyle, who has joined me in Scotland, spends the day traipsing around the town, trying to find a therapist who will give me a massage for free. He manages to find one, and as soon as I'm told someone is going to touch my legs, I think: 'Everything is going to be OK again.' By touching my legs, she touches my mind. Suddenly, something inside me is imploring me to forget all that nonsense about quitting, man up and just keep going.

Somewhat healed, I have a long, hard word with myself. I tell myself never to get cocky and over-confident again. I need to look at the rest of the Challenge logically and strategically, without too much emotion. I'll add on extra miles when I feel like it; on the days I don't, I won't. I'll walk when I need to, become more selfish. At times, it has to be about me rather than other people, because it's me who has to get to the end.

• • • • • • • • • •

INSPIRATION OF THE WEEK – RUN THAT BY US AGAIN!

SUNDAY MIRROR, 26 JUNE 2016

'...Ben now plans to jog an extra 2.5 miles every day to make sure he completes 10,506 miles in 401 days as planned. Ben said: "We've got our work cut out, but I'm feeling positive..."'

CHAPTER 11

Falling Apart

The Challenge was 24 hours a day, seven days a week; up at six, to bed at 11, constantly on the go in between; doing school visits in the morning, introducing myself to new people before each marathon, all wanting pictures, all asking the same questions for the next six hours, questions I'd heard thousands of times before. My answers were getting shorter and shorter, although I still had to make sure the people asking them were happy and comfortable and enjoying the experience. After each marathon, my massage therapist would ask all the same questions again, and I'd be asked all the same questions again when I finally got to my accommodation, maybe two or three times over if they had kids. Add in social media, media interviews, and it all became mentally exhausting, especially when we were approaching 300 marathons. It was lovely that they were all interested, and it might seem churlish to complain about it, but sometimes I just wanted to shut off from the world for the sake of my sanity.

It got to the point where we were being offered a huge amount of free accommodation, but I couldn't bring myself to stay with people. So I told Dad and Kyle that I'd stay with people two days a week because I wanted to maintain that connection, but that the rest of the time I needed to be on my own. The other options available to us were campsites or low-budget hotels (I spent one night in a car park in Bodmin on day 16, and felt scared, like a sitting duck, because the branding on Florence wasn't exactly subtle), but we still had to find money for them, and we'd pretty much run out. All the cash from the sale of my house and possessions had gone, and it wasn't just accommodation we needed money for, but also food (remember, I was putting away anything between 5–6,000 calories a day, about twice the recommended average), petrol (£90 a tank) and new 401 merchandise. So in July, after my 310th marathon in Fort William, in the Scottish Highlands, I put a video out and made a direct plea for financial help. I'd resisted it and discussed it with the team at length, because I did feel a bit guilty asking for money and never wanted to beg. But I had to be pragmatic and honest about it – I needed to do everything in my power to complete the Challenge and this was the only way that was going to happen. I couldn't have lived with myself if the Challenge had failed because it ran out of funding, because so many people had invested so much to get to this point, and not just the 401 team.

. . . .

Joanne Gould, one of the 401 notorious travellers: *I ran with Ben 12 times during the Challenge, all marathons apart from one. The first time was Milton Keynes, on 6 April 2016. Because I'm not a confident person, I was really nervous. So on the way there, I said to my husband: 'I can't do this, I need to go back.' It had nothing to do with the running, because I love running, it was to do with the fact that I'm quite shy about meeting new people. My husband persuaded me to go through with it, and I'm so glad he did. When I got there, Ben was standing in the car park. I said hello and told him I was really out of my comfort zone. He was just so lovely, introduced me to everybody, and throughout the day he kept on checking I was OK. He was the one running 401 marathons, there were lots of people there apart from me, but he just made everybody feel included.*

That first marathon was a really big deal for me, but running with Ben made me feel like I was part of something special. By extension, it made me feel special about myself, and that gave me more confidence. By the end, I was travelling across the country, on my own, meeting hundreds of new people. I'm 51 now, but meeting Ben changed how I look at myself. Ben taught me that it's never too late to do something different; that you can overcome anything and achieve great things; and that by changing who you are, you can help change other people's lives as well.

. . . .

Instead of setting up a GoFundMe page and asking for cash directly, I gave our 401 merchandise an extra push – T-shirts, hoodies, vests, wristbands – linked to the online shop and asked people to share it with as many people as possible. Luckily, the video got a lot of attention and had the desired effect. We had created our own 401 retail outlet and Kyle's mum and dad, Pat and Colin, pretty much ran it on their own, for which I'm forever grateful. They were packing envelopes and parcels from their home near Blackpool and sent out almost £50,000-worth of merchandise during the course of the Challenge (although after costs taken out, we were left with about £10,000). They sent me a picture once, and all you could see were Pat's eyes peering through this pile of parcels. Their living room looked like a sweatshop!

But we weren't just struggling financially, the whole thing felt like it was falling apart. Not only did Dad end up in hospital with kidney stones – at the same time as Mum, who had had the first of many hip replacements, on top of her illness – but Tolu was managing a bar by night, managing The 401 Challenge by day and almost falling to pieces. We got a lady called Lucy Saunders, a friend of Vicky Burr, to help handle some of the PR, and Kyle became even more important, having come on board full-time in March, after quitting his PhD and moving back in with his mum and dad in Preston. We were also starting to plan the final few days – what were we going to do to make sure it finished with a bang? Put it this way, everyone became stretched to their limits and started to have little shirty moments with each other. One of the team would disappear for a few days to cool off, and I'm sure they all felt like quitting from time to time. I understood why, because they were exhausted, like me. And when you're exhausted, you're emotional, and things can get blown out of proportion.

. . . .

Tolu Osinnowo, 401 project manager: *It wasn't all rosy and there were times when I wanted to kill Ben. He'd text me and say: 'I was running with this guy the other day and he told me he hadn't received his 401 T-shirt.' And I'd be thinking: 'I'm shipping out merchandise every single day, responding to press enquiries, helping you update social media, driving my housemates mad by editing videos – which at one point meant playing "Runnin'" by Beyoncé about 500 times in a row – stop telling me about some bloke who hasn't received his T-shirt!'*

There would be massive problems going on behind the scenes, when we didn't have a route planned, or we'd been booked by two schools on the same day, or another school had cancelled, but we never wanted to tell Ben about any of those things because he's one of those people who takes everybody else's problems on board. At one point we had to take him off the 401 email chain because he was trying to get involved. We had to tell him: 'All you need to do is focus on running, keep yourself healthy and keep telling people why you're doing what you're doing.'

I was working Wednesday to Sunday at the bar, but because the bar was attached to a hotel that didn't have a manager, I sometimes had to take on that role as well. Sometimes I'd start work at six in the evening and get home at four or five in the morning, before getting up a few hours later to answer emails about the 401. Towards the end of the Challenge, I felt like quitting. I was so inspired by what Ben was doing, so wanted to be a part of it and make sure it was a success, I was determined to be there at the end. But one of the things I learnt was that you have to look after yourself, otherwise you're not going to be of any help to anyone else.

The week after my 30th birthday, there were issues going on with my bar – sewage pipes exploding in the middle of the dancefloor, licensing issues – and I was also trying to organise the final marathon, which we wanted to be this all-singing, all-dancing event, and I started falling to pieces. Kyle came down to Brighton, sat me down and told me I needed to take a break, before reporting back to Ben. It was like a full-scale intervention. Ben made me see it was OK to admit that I wasn't OK. He also told me that they loved me, that I was one of their closest friends, but that they loved me more than the project and wanted me to be OK. I grew up in foster care and didn't always have people telling me that they cared about me, so Ben and Kyle telling me those things was just so nice. So I took a break and sought help.

* * * * * * * * * *

Although it might sound heartless, I didn't feel guilty about affecting other people's lives so much. I didn't even feel responsible for Dad's kidney stones, even though I'm pretty sure they were a result of the sheer stress he was under, having to do an 80-mile round trip to see Mum every day in hospital in Nottingham, while organising accommodation and routes for me. I don't think I was selfish before the Challenge, but I learned to be. People think being selfish is a bad thing, but I don't necessarily agree: if you want to achieve what is viewed as the impossible, you have to be a bit selfish sometimes. The team was ensuring the project would be a success, and in order for that to happen, they had to keep me happy. Everybody came aboard of their own free will and they were all aware of what was needed to complete the project. And, luckily, it never happened that everybody wanted to give up at the same time.

Lots of things went wrong, and we weren't prepared for a lot of it, despite Dad's stellar 60-page contingency dossier. Dad might have turned their dining room into a command centre, but he was the only person in it, everyone else was dotted all over the country. Most of the time, all I really had to do was wake up in the morning and think: 'Right, this is what I've got to do today.' All the information was downloaded for me onto Google Calendar, so I knew exactly where I was running, who I was running with, where I was staying, where the therapist was, all the times and contact details. But it's like that old military quote: 'A plan only survives first contact'. You can plan to the nth degree, but nobody had ever done anything on this scale before and the Challenge was constantly evolving, so we were always having to react to things.

Even with his background in operational management, I'm sure Dad learnt a lot – dealing with running clubs is not like dealing with officers in the RAF. There's a hierarchy in the forces: if you ask for something, it gets done. Asking normal civilians to do things can be frustrating for a military man, because normal civilians don't have to obey requests, or might just ignore you completely. Dad will always make things happen eventually because he's a fixer, but it was Kyle who held the whole thing together; he was the glue. Even when things were getting fractious elsewhere, his relationship with Tolu held fast. He's also highly organised and his ability to process a vast amount of information, accurately, is phenomenal. So while so much went wrong, I couldn't have had a better team to make things right again. I can honestly say that without them this project wouldn't have succeeded.

Presumably, because editors still didn't think I'd complete it, even when I was approaching the 300-day point, they were still reluctant to commit man hours, time, money and column inches to the story. So Lucy Saunders came up with a plan to create renewed press attention by focusing more on the personal aspect of the Challenge. Most of the time, I turned up at a town, met some people, did a marathon and left. Hopefully, people in that town were inspired, but because I was living in my own bubble and always off to the next place, I didn't really get an idea of how much it was affecting people. As a result of Lucy's brainwave, we started a social media campaign, asking people to send in their experiences of the project and how it had inspired them. We were soon inundated, and their stories gave the project added depth, which in turn gave the press something to get their teeth into.

• • • • • • • • • •

Katie Russell, Ben's biggest fan: *The first time I met Ben was at the Bournemouth Marathon in 2015. I was supporting my mum, saw him running along with this big 401 flag on his back and we took a selfie together. But the first time we had a proper chat was when he came to Newbury on day 65. He* *was such a character, very kind, warm and friendly. And he made me feel like I wasn't alone. When you end up in a dark place, it doesn't matter how much your mum tells you you're not the only one going through it, you still don't quite believe it. But when Ben was talking about things that happened in his past, I was thinking: 'Oh my God, that's what I'm feeling right now. There's actually someone else like me.' It was the first time I'd felt like anybody had really understood me. That was such a nice feeling.*

A few years ago, when I was 15, things got quite sour at school. No one should expect to be bullied, but if you can understand why it's happening, you can at least rationalise it. But I couldn't understand why they were making me feel like that. It started out with petty things. When they walked past they'd call me names. They'd stand around me in the corridor and make me feel really uncomfortable. The names got worse and suddenly even people who weren't bullying me were pointing at me and talking. It just grew and grew. The lowest of my low points was when they sent letters to my house, full of horrific stuff about me and my family. I had health difficulties, psychosomatic issues to do with my back, which I believe stemmed from the bullying. It got to the point where I didn't want to go to school anymore and I hardly left the house. And I thought to myself: 'What's the point in living?' I couldn't see any positives in my life. The only thing that kept me going was my family. But when you're that low, you don't even want your family to see you like that. You think: 'They'd be better off without me.'

I'd had a lot of medical help and none of it really changed anything. I found it so hard to talk to anyone about it, because I didn't want to face my emotions and break down. So I held it all in. But Ben was a far greater help than any counsellor had been. He didn't know me, so he could have just said, 'Sorry about that,' and left it at that. But he listened and understood. He was able to say: 'Yeah, I've been through that.' It wasn't that Ben advised me what to do, but I knew I wasn't just talking to a blank wall. He wasn't doing it because it was his job and he was getting paid to do it, he was doing it because he wanted to.

Running is a huge thing in my family. My mum, dad and brother have done so much running to raise money for charity and I'd always go and support them. But I never thought I would ever run because I had such a block in my head from the bullying. I just thought: 'Why would I be able to do that?' I just had no belief. When I met him for the first time, he said: 'Are you going to come and run the last mile then?' He said it like he was joking, but even so I said: 'No chance.' He did an assembly for some of the lower years at my school and I stood at the back and listened, and afterwards I thought: 'Actually, why can't I do that?' So when it got to the last mile, I thought: 'You know what? I'm gonna do it, I'm gonna do it...'

It was the hardest thing I've ever done in my life, but I still did it. The feeling was overwhelming. I was ecstatic, so proud. But at the same time, it was hard for me because I didn't feel like I was allowed to be proud of myself. Even if I baked a cake and it turned out well, I didn't feel like I could give myself credit. The bullies took that away from me. But now I'd run that last mile, I thought: 'Why can't I unblock other things in my head? Leaving the house, going into town, watching my brother play football again.' It sounds like little things, but it was major stuff for me. It was overcoming little things like that that *eventually got me to university. And it was Ben who changed my mindset.*

Sarah Russell, Katie's grateful mum: *When I read why Ben was doing The 401 Challenge, I was like, 'Oh my God, if there is anything I can do to support this chap, I've got to do it!' I got in touch and ended up organising the run for him in Newbury. I got the school to do an assembly, for Years seven and eight – they ran around the school with him and then we went off and did the rest of it. I just really hit it off with him, struck up a friendship immediately. He was just such a genuine person, I don't think I'd ever met anyone I'd felt so comfortable with.*

From about the age of 11, Katie was getting a lot of pains in her back, and we were taking her to lots of places and basically nobody believed her, which triggered lots of issues. Eventually she had an MRI scan and they discovered she had ovarian cysts. But then she started getting bullied by kids at school, because they thought she was making things up as well. She had her operation and the pain went, but the bullying got worse, so she developed a psychosomatic disorder, which meant she was feeling real pain, even though the thing that was causing that pain had gone. I found it really hard to understand, I couldn't get how something that was just in her mind could be real pain.

She used to do gymnastics, dancing, trampolining, but everything stopped. She wouldn't exercise, wouldn't do anything, because she didn't have any confidence. She barely went to school for a year and barely left her room for three months. When I explained all this to Ben, he got it, because he'd been in her shoes. He explained how she was feeling, how she saw things, and that helped me understand her and how to deal with it. So many people have read the textbooks, but they don't really understand. The medical world could learn loads from Ben, not least that everybody is different and you've got to treat them as individuals.

She came along that day in Newbury, with my mum and dad, to support Ben. They were driving around, and the next minute Katie got out of the car and said: 'I'm gonna do a bit of running.' I was like, 'You're what?!' I don't know what Ben said to her, but she ended up running a mile. She cried the whole way, but he ran with her and got her to the finish line. I ran with him about 10 times, and when he came back to Newbury, he came and stayed with us and Katie decided she wanted to run again. But just before, she got herself into a bit of a state, saying she didn't think she could do it. Ben took her aside, had a little chat, and the next thing they appeared, hand in hand, and she ended up running something like three miles. I don't know what he said, but whatever it was, it worked. That's an incredible power to have, to be able to give somebody the belief that they can do something.

• • • • • • • • • •

JUNE 2016 IN NUMBERS
Marathons: **20**
Miles run: **548.1** (average per day: **27.4**)
Running time: **111:03.18** hours (average per day: **5:33.09**)
Number of people run with: **358**
Distance personal bests: **41**
First marathons/ultra-marathons: **19**
Pints of cider: **15**
Flat whites: **30**

• • • • • • • • • •

DAYS 297–316: Kyle joins me for two weeks, which really helps, and I pass the 300-marathon mark in John o'Groats, on the way from Duncansby Head to Dunnet Head. There isn't a massive reception or anything, just a few people I'd run with before, but it's a big symbolic moment. The view of the Orkney Isles is simply stunning, and looking out to sea, I remember how I felt in Land's End, 260 days earlier, and how far away from my goal I seemed back then.

Travelling back down the A9 towards Inverness again, it feels like I'm almost on the home straight. To Ullapool for day 307, and we also visit Achiltibuie, one of the UK's most isolated places, which overlooks Badentarbet Bay to the west, Loch Broom and the Summer Isles to the south. More importantly, a young lad running with me completes his first marathon that day. It's back to Strathpeffer for day 308, then onto Drumnadrochit, running on the amazing but hilly Great Glen Way. After arriving in Fort William, I run part of the Caledonian Canal, before a guy from Mountain Rescue leads me through the foothills of Ben Nevis. The whole time I'm thinking: 'Dad! What the hell have you done?' But, my God, I'm glad I did it. On to the magical Glencoe, where a wild stag eats food out of my hand, we have to negotiate fields filled with cows and scramble over electric fences. Along the West Highland Way, I see where scenes from the James Bond film *Skyfall* were filmed and Jim and Trish, who have planned my route that day, present me with a tuxedo T-shirt, a Martini and a toy Aston Martin.

I run 70 days in Scotland throughout the Challenge, and about 2000 miles. Not only that, but 25 people join me to run ultra-marathons for the first time, because that's almost all I was doing after my back injury. When, for whatever reason, running clubs don't extend the route as we'd asked them to do, I just do loops and pick up guys at the back, so I'm still getting the extra miles in. This also means I get to run with everybody, so it fits the project perfectly. But there's no getting away from the fact that Scotland has turned into a tough old slog. My back hurts like hell, I'm tired, I've got a cold, I look like crap and I walk a lot of it, because it's incredibly hilly and basically off-road. I'm grumpy, I don't want to talk to anybody and just want to go home.

Dad is contacting running clubs to let them know the state I'm in, telling them I've got a back issue and that the main goal is just to get me to the end, but I get the feeling some clubs want to test me. I always run what I'm given, but it takes me to the absolute limit. Having just crossed the Erskine Bridge, and the day before my run to Port Glasgow on day 316, I finally take the trimmer to my beard in Greenock. I feel like crap, look a mess and have become convinced I'm scaring kids. Maybe it's a sub-consciously symbolic gesture of purification. On the downside, I now look like a 12-year-old.

CHAPTER 12

A Very Wonderful Adventure

When I put a video out announcing that pre-registration is open for the 401ˢᵗ and final marathon, it isn't like I can see the finish line, but at least it feels like there is one. We actually started planning marathon number 401 at about the 250 mark, and it was Kyle and Tolu who did most of the work. We decided we were going to hold a big event in Bristol, but big events mean insurance and licences and council approval, as well as balloons and inflatables. When it became apparent that an event of that size would cost a hell of a lot of money – when the whole point was to raise money, not spend it – we decided to make the live event secondary and a virtual event the primary focus in the hope that we'd get thousands of people running with us and raising money on that final day, all over the world.

. . . .

Anji Andrews, kindred spirit: *At first, I didn't even know why Ben was doing what he was doing, I was just interested in this guy who wanted to push himself to the limit. I work for Allison Curbishley and Steve Cram's events company, and the first time I met Ben was on his birthday, when he was running in Durham. My husband Paul ran just over half of the marathon with him, while I only ran about three miles, because I had a bit of an ankle injury. I was doing a bit of fundraising myself, for a friend who had recently died of cancer at the age of 36, and was selling wristbands with his* name on – 'Run for Marcus'. I asked Ben if he'd wear one, and he wore it for the rest of the Challenge, which I thought was a special thing to do.

Every time he was in my area, I was either at work or had other commitments, but I kept an eye on him. My dad had been unwell with cancer for a couple of years, before eventually declining over a short space of time. The day he died was the same day Ben announced he'd had to halt the Challenge because of his back injury. I shared Ben's video with friends and they must have thought: 'This is a bit weird, her dad's just died and she's sharing videos about this guy she hardly knows.' But I really connected with Ben that day, because I was suffering all this pain, while he had made this huge decision. And when Ben sent me a message of consolation, that was such a massive thing for me, because he had all of this bad stuff going on.

In the weeks after I lost my dad, I did a lot of running. Running doesn't heal everything, but it gives you time to work things out, or not if you don't want to. My dad would have understood that, because he was a very fit and active person before he got cancer. And I remember thinking: 'As soon as the Challenge restarts, I'm going to run a marathon with Ben.' Things were just so dark and difficult, I needed something positive to get involved in. Eventually I did go and do one of Ben's marathons, in Leeds on day 340, with my husband Paul. And I always say that in such a dark year, in which I lost my good friend and my dad, that day in Leeds was a ray of light.

Running with Ben was like a counselling session on the hoof. I had a long conversation with him about my loss, because I knew he'd understand. After about 22 miles, my *calf seized up, and Ben said: 'There is a shortcut back, Anji. Nobody will judge you if you don't do the full distance.' I thought: 'No chance. Absolutely not.' The last words my dad ever said to me were: 'Never, ever give up.' So I said to Ben: 'This is one of those moments where I'm going to draw on what my dad told me.' I walked the rest of the way, but I finished it.*

That day helped change my outlook on running. I'd always been super-competitive, everything had always been about times. But running has become more a form of therapy for me. That day in Leeds was by far the slowest marathon I've ever done – but it was one of my biggest achievements. You don't have to run fast, it's about what it means to you.

· · · · · · · · · ·

JULY 2016 IN NUMBERS
Marathons: **31**
Miles run: **871.8** (average per day: **28.1**)
Running time: **177:35.00** hours (average per day: **5:43.43**)
Number of people run with: **672**
Distance personal bests: **152**
First marathons/ultra-marathons: **58**
Pints of cider: **16**
Flat whites: **31**

· · · · · · · · · ·

401 MARATHON MAN RUNS ROUTE WITH SETTLE HARRIERS

CRAVEN HERALD, 9 AUGUST 2016

'...Twenty-four runners, aged from nine to 64, accompanied Ben for various parts of the route, with three runners accompanying him for the full distance...'

· · · · · · · · · ·

DAYS 317–345: In Hull, on day 343, a lovely guy called Lucas Meagor, who I met the last time I was running in the area in January, organises two marathons for me. We start at the Italia Conti school, run through the foyer, and end up going over the Humber Bridge. They actually close down one of the lanes and we run through a toll booth!

Day 345 in Scunthorpe, which I thought would be quiet, turns out to be our busiest day so far. An incredible 278 people come out to run and reporters and TV crews are now a common sight. This adds another dynamic. Journalists have started turning up unannounced and I'm having to do interviews before I start running, which can potentially push everything out of sync. As such, it's becoming more and more difficult to keep control of events. But it would be churlish to complain. We've worked so hard to build interest, so it's nice that they are starting to think that I might actually do it. All those thousands of testimonials we asked for, which have been sent out to the media, are starting to have another effect: rather than it simply being a story about some madman running 401 marathons in 401 days, it's become a lot more textured.

· · · · · · · · · ·

Mandy Newton, Ben's heroine: *I didn't know the details of Ben's story until quite a bit later – about the bullying, the depression, the attempts on his own life. He really was in a bad place. I've got a beautiful family and they're my inspiration, the reason I get up every day. But I do remember that when I was a teenager, I didn't feel I had much to live for, either. So I don't judge people, I just think how awful it must be to feel that low and that empty.*

We're both labelled and pre-judged before people have even spoken to us. People can see my 'difference', because I'm in a wheelchair. Some people can't work out if I have learning disabilities, so they'll decide not to talk to me. Other times, they will talk to the people I'm with rather than to me. People can't see Ben's sexuality, but when they find out, they expect it to define him. But he is who he is, an amazing person, regardless of his sexuality. I learnt from Ben that you shouldn't be afraid of being yourself, whatever you are; to banish doubts; always follow your dreams. It doesn't matter what your background is, what colour you are, what your sexuality is, what your apparent abilities or disabilities are, just be who you are and be proud of that.

Our backgrounds don't seem alike, but there is a real overlap in our experiences. Because Ben tried to take his own life, he knows more than most people how precious life is. Doing the Challenge must have made him think: 'Friggin' Nora, thank God I didn't succeed in killing myself, because look what I'm doing now!' He didn't stay in that pit, he somehow mustered the strength to crawl out of it and do the amazing things he's doing now. And because he's so human, he gives hope to everybody. Sometimes people say to me: 'You've never hit rock bottom, because you've never wanted to give up or kill yourself.' But

I was in the same boat as Ben. My accident came at a very bad time in my children's lives. My little one had just started secondary school, another had just started GCSEs and another was doing his A-levels, and they really resented me for a while. One of them actually said: 'I hate my new mum, I want my old mum back.'

I was an avid runner, but couldn't do that anymore after the accident. It was Sod's Law – the one thing I would have done to help me deal with a dreadful situation was the one thing I now couldn't do. Ben used to tell me that whenever he was having dark moments during the Challenge, he would think of me and how lucky he was that he could run at all. But thank God I didn't die in that accident, because I've still got so much to live for. My children are blown away by me now, they can't believe the things that I do. One of them said to me recently: 'Mum, we're on a very wonderful adventure with you…'

I saw Ben again at the Brighton Marathon, when I fell out of my wheelchair trying to hug him. Ben was shouting: 'Help her! Help her! Get her back up!' He's just so human, so comfortable in his own skin. What you see is what you get, which is a real irony when you think about how he hid who he really was for so long. He's a very special man and has had a massive impact on me. I'm so glad I had the privilege of meeting him and can call him a true friend.

Nick Dransfield, Ben's running brother: *Almost every day he'd have people shaking his hands and crying on him, saying: 'I never thought I'd do a marathon, and today I've done one.' People would rock up and say: 'I gave up smoking a few weeks ago, just to come along and run with you for five or 10km.' We'd be like, 'Really? OK, let's see how this* goes…' To have that sort of effect on people is astonishing. He acted as a bridge to a better life, and I used to joke that he was the Jesus of running, going around the country preaching: 'Look, you can do it if you really want it enough!' Sure enough, lots of people did.

I'd never done back-to-back marathons before I did them with him. People were telling me I was mad, but I said: 'This guy's done hundreds, surely I can do five!' In fact, that could have been his motto: 'If I've done 401 marathons, surely you can do one!' Running helped me lose weight, made me healthier and I always enjoyed the competitive aspect of it. It was a way of showing my kids that physical activity is a good thing. But Ben has changed my focus, he just has that effect on people. He's made me think more about giving back. I've got into pacing at official events, big races like the Liverpool Marathon. I like marshalling, helping other runners out, assisting in any way I can. I think it's fair to say that Ben has made me less selfish.

. . . .

RUNNER BACK IN BRISTOL FOR 371st MARATHON

BRISTOL EVENING POST, 6 SEPTEMBER 2016

'…I've been counting down the days. It has been a crazy one, and it'll be nice to be back home…'

. . . .

DAYS 346–372: My visit to RAF Cranwell on day 346 is emotional. It's the home of officer training, not far from Lincoln, and a place very close to Dad's heart. I run around the airbase a few times, and at the very end the cadets give me a guard of honour; I run up the steps of the officers' building, which people aren't normally allowed to do, and at the top I'm greeted by the Air Commodore. My dad is there and I can see how proud he is of me. The RAF was such a big part of his life, so it means a lot to him, and therefore to me. And because I can see he's emotional, I'm emotional, too. People often ask me who my hero is, and I always say it's Dad. So to be able to give him that experience means a lot.

· · · · · · · · · ·

AUGUST 2016 IN NUMBERS
Marathons: **31**
Miles run: **878.1** (average per day: **28.3**)
Running time: **190:37.34** hours (average per day: **6:08.57**)
Number of people run with: **1625**
Distance personal bests: **308**
First marathons/ultra-marathons: **120**
Pints of cider: **16**
Flat whites: **31**

On to Manchester for the final time on day 352, then back into Wales. Wales isn't a place I have explored much, but definitely somewhere I want to go back to. The people are friendly and supportive – I was never on my own – and the scenery, especially around the outside of the country, is spectacular. But much as I love Wales, I'm counting down the days to crossing the Severn Bridge and getting back to Bristol, before I leave again for the final backwards-shaped C that will bring me back home for days 400 and 401. When I do return to Bristol for the first time in 372 days, it's wonderful to be home, but there are more practical reasons for returning: we've made the decision to move back to Portishead, so Kyle has had to commute from Preston to look at flats. The problem is, nobody will let us put a rental deposit down on anything because I need to view the properties as well and, obviously, I've been out running. Even though we explain our rather bizarre circumstances, it falls on deaf ears – so now, on top of everything else, I'm having to go flat hunting!

The 401 Challenge is coming to what we hope will be a memorable end, but I'm still having to deal with everything that normal people living normal lives have to deal with. The plan is to leave Bristol, curve down into Hampshire and run along the south coast, before coming back to Bristol for the final couple of days. And people are saying to me: 'When it gets to 20 days to go, you'll be able to start the final countdown.' And I'll say: 'What if someone told you that tomorrow, they were going to start running 20 marathons in 20 days? Would you think they were close to the finish line?! Of course not! You'd think they were mad.'

· · · · · · · · · ·

PORTSMOUTH JOGGERS HELP MARATHON MAN BEN FINISH 392nd RUN

THE PORTSMOUTH NEWS, 27 SEPTEMBER 2016

'…Those running included Irene Pollard, 73, who is battling breast cancer. She said: "Ben's fantastic…"'

· · · · · · · · · ·

DAYS 373–400: Fourteen days from the end, we've raised £160,000, but are still £90,000 short of our target, so it's time for more pleas. So I put out another video, asking for more stories from people who have been involved with the Challenge, which we can then use to interest the media. I post a 401 Donut Challenge, asking people to attempt to eat a donut without licking their lips and donate a fiver if they can't. Anything that might raise a few quid, I'll do (although I can never quite do the Donut Challenge without licking my lips!).

In Southampton, on day 393, I'm interviewed by Heart Radio on the hoof, while in Winchester, on day 394, the kids from St Faith's Primary School line part of the route. I'm proud to be asked to sound the klaxon to start the Bournemouth Marathon on day 398, which I'm running for the second time in the Challenge, and I'm back in Bristol for marathon 399. The good news is, we've finally found a new home and Kyle has already moved in. The bad news is, we're going to have to sleep on the floor because I sold all my furniture and we don't have any money to buy new stuff. That's one way of staying grounded…

* * * * * * * * * *

SEPTEMBER 2016 IN NUMBERS
Marathons: **30**
Miles run: **806.3** (average per day: **26.9**)
Running time: **184:30.47** hours (average per day: **6:09.02**)
Number of people run with: **1214**
Distance personal bests: **175**
First marathons/ultra-marathons: **69**
Pints of cider: **15**
Flat whites: **30**

* * * * * * * * * *

Jim and Trish Divine, two of Scotland's finest: *We never had any doubts that Ben would do it. After our first day running with him, we saw him first thing in the morning and he was bouncing about like Tigger, ready to go again, and this was after he'd run 100-odd marathons. Nothing was going to stop him. We'd both done athletics and met people who had reached great heights in the sport, so we kept trying to tell Ben that he was given a gift, because we didn't think he knew it. Not everybody can just decide to become an endurance runner, but if he put his mind to it, he could break three hours for the marathon, no problem. Not everyone is capable of doing what he did – you have to have an enormous engine, as well as the mental strength. We'd never seen mental toughness like it.*

Ben was told for so many years that he wasn't gifted at anything, but it turns out he's gifted at a lot of things, not least communication. Ben taught people that it's OK to have vulnerabilities, never to give up and that anyone can do amazing things if they put their mind to it. He re-energised us, reminded us that there's much more to be done.

Nick Dransfield, Ben's running brother: *When I told people I was going to do the last 15 marathons with Ben, they thought I was mental. But I wanted a ringside seat for the end of something I don't think will ever be repeated. It broke me, mentally and physically. But Ben coached me as to how it would feel and I gained such strength from him. I also thrived on watching it all unfold in front of me. It was like watching a film that went on for two weeks, with different characters arriving and threads unfolding at different times.*

Before the Bournemouth Marathon, Ben said to me: 'I haven't had many male friends in my life, but you're one of my very best.' Thankfully, I was wearing sunglasses, because I got a bit teary and choked up. I was just very proud to think that this special man who was doing this special thing would consider me one of his best friends. From Ben, I learned that if you put your mind to something, whatever it is, you'll do it; I learned what it is to be happy; and I learned that cider from Somerset is best...

CHAPTER 13

Shall We Go Home?

I don't really sleep the night before the final marathon, and not just because I'm on a blow-up bed. I'm not emotional, it's more that I know I still have a job to do. I've achieved two of the stated goals – inspiring people and raising awareness of bullying – but I still have to finish and we're still nowhere near raising £250,000, which has become a constant source of worry. Awareness is great, but in order to capitalise on that awareness and make a difference, the charities need money more than anything.

DAY 401: The morning of the final day – 5 October 2016 – I skip breakfast before driving from Portishead to Millennium Square in Bristol, where the Challenge began 401 days earlier. It's a crisp, bright, beautiful morning, just as we'd hoped it would be. People are already setting up, including my friends, Simon and Helena Hills from TrueStart Coffee, who have stood by us through thick and thin, and Jupiter Asset Management, who made a donation on the final day and paid for the inflatable finishing arch (which don't come cheap!). Friends and family are congregating, the press start showing up, and already it's clear that I'll share this final day with more than the six people and a dog I started with.

Kyle has scheduled interviews with seemingly every journalist in the country. We've made some great contacts with *BBC Breakfast*, particularly Jon Kay, who came out to do a piece with us with seven days to go and kept the momentum going all week. Also, there on that final day are *Good Morning Britain*, BBC World News, Sky

News, BBC Radio 2, Reuters, the Press Association and some of the national newspapers, so I find myself being dragged from camera crew to camera crew, from reporter to reporter. That's my role on the final day, to be told exactly what to do. There's some butting of heads between Kyle and Dad, but otherwise it's like a well-oiled machine, just as you'd expect with those two in charge, and I'm seen and heard by tens of millions of people around the globe. It's insane for a 34-year-old from Portishead, a man who is really nothing special at all. Media satisfied, Kyle shoves me in the van and tells me to stay there for an hour, so I can get my head together. After I emerge, the crowd has swelled to hundreds and I stand on a chair to address everybody. It's such a beautiful atmosphere, a formal event run in a fun, informal way. Then, having already run 10,480 miles, I take my place on the start line, the klaxon sounds and I begin the last 26.2.

I'm still conducting live phone interviews while running, which I've done a lot over the last few weeks. The reporter or presenter can never quite believe it, because I'm never out of breath. My body has just got used to doing what I've been asking it to do. I sometimes think that it must be empowering for people to hear that the seemingly mad can seem so normal – 'If this bloke can run 401 marathons and not even be out of breath, I can do bloody anything if I put my mind to it'. That day I have about 470 people running with me, plus 2100 more in Britain and elsewhere – France, Italy, Germany, South Africa, Dubai, Hong Kong, America, Australia – via The 401 Virtual Challenge, most of them raising money for Kidscape and Stonewall. It's a mass celebration, a bringing together of like-minded people from as far afield as possible. And as the miles tick by, Twitter and Facebook start going crazy and the donations start pouring in. At the halfway point, we stop for lunch at a pub near our new flat, and somebody informs me that we've hit our target of a quarter of a million pounds. It's a massive relief, because it means we've almost achieved everything we set out to do. Sky News stick a camera in my face and I start crying. All I can think is: 'This is the most embarrassing moment of my life. What a wuss...' But once I've wiped the tears away, I allow myself to think, for the first time in 401 days, that I might just complete the Challenge. Only 13.1 miles left, a short trot back to Bristol – pull yourself together, man...

* * * * * * * * * *

Nikki Kerr, head of fundraising at Kidscape: *It was so thrilling to be involved with the Challenge, right the way through. It was great going to staff meetings and saying: 'This week we've had 'x' thousand pounds, and this many people tweeting us...' There was such a fantastic feel good factor, which I hadn't experienced before. The best thing I can do as head of fundraising is to tell people stories, and there is nothing as powerful as someone telling you their own story. Ben is brilliant at that. During the Challenge, Kidscape got frequent messages on social media, emails and the odd letter from people who had become aware of us through Ben. They wanted to share their stories with us or support what Ben was doing. And what he did is still having an impact on so many people. He brought a new awareness to Kidscape and I will forever be grateful for that.*

Before the 401, Kidscape had had four years of being in deficit. We were okay, because we'd been careful in previous years and built up some reserves. But those reserves wouldn't have lasted forever, there would have come a point where we would have had to think about cutting back on services or staff. The 401 brought us back on an even keel and then some, so we could start thinking about innovation and widening our reach and impact. We haven't used all the money Ben raised yet, because it was an awful lot. Some of it has been spent on long-running projects, like our face-to-face workshops for bullied children. We're also developing some pilot work, which will be funded by 401 money, to build resilience in young people. That fits in really well with Ben's message, that if you put your mind to something and have the right support and right skills, there is nothing you can't do. Ben thought it sounded fantastic, and signed up as a Kidscape ambassador. I won't be the first to say it and I definitely won't be the last, but Ben is an amazing man.

• • • • • • • • • •

A couple of weeks before the final day, we held a competition for a local school to run the final stretch with me. So just before the last mile, we're joined by 30 kids from Portishead Primary School. So now there are just over 500 of us, including loads of children, and it's like herding cats into a pen. Even at that stage, I hadn't really thought about the end. Suddenly, my phone rings. It's Kyle, saying: 'Where are you?! What's taking you so long? I've got the press waiting for you on the finish line, hurry up and get here!' I was like, 'I'm coming! But give me a break, I've got all these people with me!' We end up almost having a row on the phone! When I enter Millennium Square, I can't see the finish line, but suddenly I do. I run ahead of the kids, because I'm thinking: 'You know what? I've worked bloody hard, I don't want anyone crossing the line before me!' And after I cross the line, the first thing that pops into my head is: 'Oh. Is that it?'

It isn't exactly an anti-climax, because the reception is incredible. It's just different to how I thought it would be. This is the culmination of years of trials and tribulations and hard graft, and I think I'm strangely unemotional because it's all so overwhelming and frankly, I just can't deal with it. I'm surrounded by cameras and reporters and kids all chanting my name – 'Ben! Ben! Ben!' – before Kyle is pushed into the centre of the scrum and I give him a big hug and a kiss. Tolu, refreshed after her break and back on board, grabs my hand and drags me into the back of the van before all hell breaks loose. I want to celebrate with the people I ran with, have pictures taken with people who had achieved personal bests, just as I had done all the way through, but I don't get a chance to do it, because I have to do so many interviews. I do get to see Kyle's mum Pat and her mate Chez cross the finish line, having run their first ultra-marathons, despite getting lost, and I give Mum and Dad a cuddle. And if I seem unemotional, the same can't be said for Mum…

* * * * * * * * * *

Beverley Smith, Ben's mum: *We were there at the beginning, when there was a smattering of people in Millennium Square and the odd 10p was going in a bucket. But on the final day, you could hardly get in the place and there were people coming up to us with £20 notes. Towards the end, we were starting to wonder if he'd ever raise all the money, so when we heard that they'd achieved their goal, I was very, very emotional. A few hours later, when I saw him coming towards the finish line, I thought my heart was going* to burst. I was still unwell and in a wheelchair, so I couldn't get to him, and he disappeared into this crowd of people. But we eventually got to the front, and when he hugged me, I just started bawling.

People kept asking me: 'How do you feel? How do you feel?' And all I could say was: '401! 401!' I was just overwhelmed by the magnificence of his achievement. There were no other words to express how I felt. I just kept looking at him and thinking: 'That's our scraggy little kid, that broken young man, the one who thought he was useless, would never achieve anything, because he had been repeatedly told by his peers and teachers that that would be the case. But look at him now. He's like this Pied Piper character, living a life that is true, and helping others to live life like him...

Pete Smith, Ben's dad: *Occasionally, I'd see a comment on the internet along the lines of: 'How can this bloke afford to do what he's doing? Some of us have to do a job!' Normally, I couldn't be arsed replying, but once or twice I bit. I'd reply: 'I'll explain to you how he's doing what he's doing: he literally stopped his old life and sold everything – his house, every single bit of furniture, his TV, stereo – so that everything he owned was in that van, apart from one small cardboard box and a picture, which he left in our back room. And he didn't even own the van, because we paid for it. Every part of the Challenge is self-funded, he's not on benefits and he's not asking for benefits. But what he has done is something you'll never, ever do in your life – gone out and done what he wanted to do, pushed himself to the absolute limit, to raise awareness and money for a cause he is passionate about.'*

The number of people who said he wouldn't be able to do it, and he stuck two fingers up at them and did it, while having a whale of a time, most of the time. When I joined the Air Force, it was all I'd ever wanted to do, and I thoroughly enjoyed myself doing it for 40-odd years. So I was so happy that after being lost for so long, Ben was finally able to be true to himself. He was a nice man doing what he wanted to do with his life, things that made him feel good. He was finally able to say: 'Nobody is in control of me, and I can do anything I want, if I put my mind, body, heart and soul into it.' That's a powerful message for anyone.

. . . .

I take to the stage, because I want to make sure I thank Kidscape and Stonewall, who have made their presence felt on the final day. But most of all, I want to thank the members of the team who made it all possible. I did all the running, but without Kyle, Dad, Mum, Tolu, Lucy and Vicky, it never would have happened. I'm fine until I get to Kyle, and then I start to blub again. Everybody thinks I'm about to propose, but that would be too cheesy. But I just felt this outpouring of love for him. Kyle hates running, really can't stand it, but he put up with me running 401 marathons, having only been with me for a few months when I started. If that's not proof that somebody loves you, cares for you, wants the best for you in life, I don't know what is.

After the final interviews have been done, people start to shuffle off to the pub and Millennium Square soon empties. When we're finished packing up, all that is left is me, Kyle and Florence, sitting on her own in the dark. It feels symbolic, there is this overwhelming sense of: 'Oh my God, look at everything that just happened. Job done, well done, but normal life still exists. Time to get back to it….' It sounds bleak, but it's perfect. Kyle and I climb into the van and I turn to him and say: 'Shall we go home?' And we do.

· · · · · · · · · ·

Ben's Remarkable Feet!

THE DAILY EXPRESS, 6 OCTOBER 2016

'…He's worn out 23 pairs of trainers and clocked up 10,506.2 miles – the equivalent of running from London to Sydney – while enjoying the company of around 10,000 other runners and novices, plus family and friends along the way. But surely Ben's greatest accomplishment is silencing those who bullied him by crossing the finishing line yesterday having made friends and fans for life during the past 401 days…'

THE 401 CHALLENGE IN NUMBERS
Marathons: **401**
Miles run: **10,506.2** (average per day: **26.2**)
Running time: **2,145:58.58** hours (average per day: **5:21.06**)
Feet climbed: **439,637** (**15** x Mount Everest)
Calories burnt: **2.3 million**
Number of people run with: **12,697**
Distance personal bests: **1,354**
First marathons/ultra-marathons: **575**
Towns and cities visited: **292**

Facebook impressions: **36** million
School talks: **101**
Pounds raised: **330,000**
National and international awards: **12**
Pints of cider: **202**
Flat whites: **396**

CHAPTER 14

Give Me a Break

The following morning, I woke up and had back-to-back interviews for about six hours. We'd now raised about £290,000, but this was our chance to raise even more. I didn't really know what I was going to do next – we hadn't given much thought to day 402, or 403, or 404. We knew it would be an issue suddenly just stopping, but nobody had done what I'd done, so nobody could tell me how to ease back into the real world. I was flying blind. I came up with a cool-down plan, using my own logic, consisting of a month of back-to-back half-marathons, followed by a month of back-to-back 10ks, then a month of back-to-back 5ks. But the night after the end of the 401, I went out for a run, managed about eight miles and thought: 'Fuck this.' When I got home, I felt disappointed with myself, so I dragged myself out the next day, managed 11 miles and thought: 'Fuck this again. This ain't happening.' I'd done what I needed to do and now my body was saying: 'No thanks, no more.'

We were quite naïve in our understanding of how my body would react, especially my mind, and all hell broke loose. I hooked back up with my personal trainer, Andy Davis, to discover the physical effect of the Challenge on my body, and we found that all these muscles and ligaments had been weakened. My head had completely gone, there was absolutely no desire to run any distance at all. I'd been surviving on adrenaline for 401 days, but while my adrenaline levels had been through the roof, my serotonin levels had depleted, and now I just crashed through the floor. I went through a two-month period when

I wouldn't have slept at all if I hadn't been put on very strong tablets (which were actually antidepressants) because I wasn't asking my body to run through walls anymore. In fact, I wasn't really asking it to do anything. I'd lie in bed and it would feel like my heart was trying to beat a hole in my chest. It felt like somebody had stabbed me with an adrenaline needle, my body was coursing with so much energy. I started getting palpitations and when I went to get them checked out, the doctors discovered I'd lost a certain percentage of performance in my heart, although they were happy it was nothing serious.

* * * * * * * * * *

Andy Davis, Ben's personal trainer: *When I got Ben back after the Challenge was finished, he was a wreck again. Because he'd destroyed his back, he was hunched over, and I wasn't sure if it was fixable. His feet were a complete mess and his balance was shot, he couldn't even stand on one leg. He had no muscle on him, he was skin and bone, and his joints were screwed. Because of his back, we couldn't put much stress on it, so we concentrated on core stability and single leg sets, with heart-rate elevation exercises in between, because we needed to slowly bring his heart back to its previous size. We strengthened his core as much as we could and got his body back to quite a good place. But I wouldn't advise anyone to do what Ben did. Fifty marathons in a row, maybe, but certainly not 401. I don't think many people could do it anyway, even some of the fittest professional athletes. Ben told me that when he was running, he couldn't put a number on the pain. It was the mindset that got him through* *it. You have to be one of a kind to do something like that, completely and utterly driven.*

* * * * * * * * * *

My immune system was completely shot, My friend, Farah, brought the flu with her from Geneva and inadvertently passed it on to me, which compounded things. There was also the stress of wondering what was next. People kept asking me: 'What are you going to do now?' And all the while I'd be thinking: 'Please, give me a break, I need some time to process things.' I was trying to work out what the new normal was, what my new purpose in life would be, because The 401 Challenge had been my focus for so long. The antidepressants were originally to help with sleeping, but I was actually medically depressed and should have started taking them earlier.

Every day of The 401 Challenge I was giving something to somebody. And sometimes if you give too much, there isn't enough left over for you. It's like when somebody retires, people say to them: 'I bet you've been looking forward to this day?' Actually, lots of people are terrified of retirement, because they've got used to a routine and something that gives meaning to their lives, and suddenly they're thinking: 'What do I do with the next 20 or 30 years of my life?' And I found myself constantly thinking: 'Nothing I ever do will be able to match what I just did.'

* * * * * * * * * *

Beverley Smith, Ben's mum: *He was quite depressed afterwards, and it did worry me. We planned the Challenge to the nth degree, but didn't give enough thought to the* *psychological aftermath. His brother Dan was the same after his rugby career finished: he came out of something that was so focused and organised and suddenly that thing he'd been living for wasn't there anymore. So Ben must have been waking up every morning and thinking: 'Why am I even getting up? I've done it now. What's out there for me? What's my purpose?' I could relate to it, because since my accident, every day is a challenge and some days my mind isn't up to it. As a therapist, I used to say: 'If you believe you can, you will; if you believe you cannot, you never will.' But I was no good at all that last six months of the 401, which was heartbreaking for me. Thankfully he sought a doctor's help and was able to speak openly on his blog about his depression and how he'd lost his motivation to run.*

Ben is dyslexic and when he was small he'd say to me: 'Mum, I'm thick.' I'd say: 'You're not thick, Ben.' But, of course, the bullies were telling him that he was, because he couldn't spell or read as well as them. Tell someone something often enough and in the end they'll become that person. Ironically, I used to teach self-confidence classes, when I was a counsellor, but Ben often used to say to me: 'Why don't you practise what you preach?' Because I was told as a young woman that I wouldn't achieve anything either, that if I didn't learn to speak 'properly', I'd amount to nothing. But Ben will no longer let anything dictate how he wishes to live his life, and that's all part of the legacy of the 401. We love him, we've always loved him, and we'll love him whatever he does next.

* * * * * * * * * *

401

I was very aware that I didn't want to jump straight into another challenge. I'd just spent 401 days away from my family and the person I loved, and I didn't want to become one of those challenge addicts. I wanted to make sure that what I had achieved was consolidated, not dribbled away, and used to do good in the future.

I quickly decided I wasn't going to do the cool-down as planned, mainly because I'd lost my love of running, which was both a shock and not all that surprising. I'd run 10,506.2 miles in 401 days, put my body through hell, so running was no longer a way of expressing myself, or of de-stressing and clearing my mind. I ran with my local running club a few times, but because it had become so normal, it had become mundane. It wasn't about finding a replacement as such, because I hoped my love of running would come back, once I was in the right place again. So I took to cross-training instead, which is essentially various fitness classes. Unlike relationships, which you can't really put on hold indefinitely, you can take running back up when you feel like it. More pressing was establishing a new life and reintegrating myself into society. I had hoped people would take things out of our hands and come to us with all these wonderful plans and ideas, but reality soon set in and I realised we were going to have to build something new from scratch all on our own. I could use The 401 Challenge as the framework for that something new, but I couldn't dine out on it forever, and didn't want to.

We knew we had a short time to capitalise on the 401 buzz before creating something else for the press to write about, so I couldn't really disappear on holiday for four weeks and chill. We'd won a few awards during the Challenge, and it's always nice to be recognised because it shows that what you did must have been positive. But I was still completely shell-shocked when I was invited to Pride of Britain a few weeks after the Challenge finished, where we won the ITV Fundraiser of the Year award. I was interviewed on TV with a couple of the actors from *Cold Feet*, John Thompson and Fay Ripley, and they said some lovely things about me. But I'm not very comfortable at those glitzy, celebrity events because to me it doesn't seem like reality.

I met Theresa May at Number 10, where we spoke about LGBT rights on the patio, and also about her penchant for shoes. I could tell I was just another slot in her schedule, but she was actually really nice. I could relate to her manner, because that's how I've learned to be sometimes – short and sharp, because I'm always moving on to the next thing. I was also invited by Comic Relief to go to the Queen's Young Leaders Awards at Buckingham Palace. I'm a huge royalist, so I was very honoured. Six of us were picked to meet the Queen in a private line-up. She asked what it was I did, I told her, and she replied: 'Oh yes, I read about you, you're a little bit crazy...' I was so thrown by meeting her that I turned straight to Prince Harry and said: 'Oh, alright, mate, how you doing?' He smiled, thank God.

Straight afterwards, I was driven to the Australian High Commission for a dinner. Kyle wasn't with me, and I didn't know how to behave. I was thinking: 'Do I approach people? Just jump into conversations? What happens if they start talking about politics? I don't have a clue about anything like that.' So I grabbed a glass of champagne, went down to the basement and sat on the toilet for 25 minutes. I came up just in time for dinner and left straight afterwards. And having dipped my toe into that world, I feel like I don't need to do it anymore. Kyle loves all that stuff, he's really good at it. When the Lawn Tennis Association invited us to Wimbledon to show their appreciation for what I'd achieved, Kyle had to tell me: 'Saying no is not an option. You're doing this for me, because I did all of that stuff for you.' We had Centre Court tickets and saw Andy Murray and Rafael Nadal, it was a great day. But I don't do things anymore that I don't have an interest in. I know what I like, and I'd rather focus on that, rather than things I don't enjoy.

When I woke up on the morning of the BBC Sports Personality of the Year awards, in December 2016, I really didn't want to go. And I mean I *really* didn't want to go. I was crying on the sofa, had no control over my emotions. I didn't want to be that person who had run 401 marathons anymore. I was in a pit of depression, couldn't drag myself out of bed or wash myself most days. I just felt so lost and had no energy to be nice to people anymore and promote what I'd done. It wasn't as if I was bored of talking about it, I always retained the passion, but I was simply spent. So putting on a suit, standing in front of millions of people and giving a speech was very low on the list of things I wanted to do. Luckily, Kyle stuck with me, remained my rock throughout. We laugh about it now. He says to me: 'When you finished the Challenge, I thought it was all going to be shiny and rosy, but it turned out to be the worst couple of months ever!'

The BBC sent a car to Portishead to pick us up, by which time I'd managed to pull myself together, and the night ended up being incredible. It wasn't so much the amount of people who were there, it was that people had decided I was worthy of a Sports Personality award. I kept thinking: 'Me? Sport? Personality?' To me, Sports Personality was about people like Jessica Ennis-Hill, Andy Murray and Muhammad Ali. But it was lovely that people thought I was worthy of receiving something, especially when I found out more about Helen Rollason, for whom the award was named. Helen was the first female presenter of BBC *Grandstand*, but died in 1999 after a two-year battle with cancer. During those two years, she helped raise over £5m for a new cancer wing at the North Middlesex Hospital, which is why her award is given for 'outstanding achievement in the face of adversity'. There just seemed to be so much love for her at the BBC.

We arrived in Birmingham and had some lunch with Allison Curbishley, Steve Cram and Paula Radcliffe. I'd met Paula a couple of times but was still star-struck. The whole time I was thinking: 'Keep it cool, Ben, keep it cool...' But she was very nice and down to earth. I got suited and booted, and when I arrived at the Genting Arena, nobody from the press wanted to talk to me, because none of them knew who I was! And when I walked in, I looked up, saw 12,000 people and thought: 'Oh shit...' There were all these famous faces – Prince William, the Brownlee brothers, Michael Phelps – and I felt like a nobody. I was petrified, absolutely shitting myself for the entire show.

When they started introducing my section, I could feel the butterflies and sickness start to build inside me. I looked at Kyle, he put his hand on my knee, and I noticed people looking at me, probably thinking: 'Oh, that's why this bloke is here...' My video came on, which showed me running on the seafront in Brighton, and the music kicked in – 'Rise Up' by Andra Day, which absolutely kills me every time I hear it – and I was gone. I bowed my head and desperately tried to compose myself, while Kyle's grip on my knee grew gradually tighter. Then a load of members of Birmingham's Kings Heath Running Club started pouring in, all wearing 401 running gear, and I looked at Kyle and said: 'You bastard.'

I was an emotional wreck and the walk to the stage, flanked by the Kings Heath guys, all clapping and cheering, was a complete blur. I couldn't look up, because I knew that if I made eye contact with anyone I'd lose it completely and be standing on stage, in front of 12,000 people and millions of viewers watching on TV, blubbing my eyes out. It would have made for great TV, but I wanted to keep my dignity. The stage was packed with stars. Tom Daley gave me a hug, so did Paula Radcliffe, who also reminded me to breathe. Good advice! Clare Balding and Gabby Logan handed me the award, which is a beautiful thing, by the way, and when the applause died down, I started speaking, while somehow managing to hold things together. Just about. I didn't know what I was going to say, but I knew I didn't want to bang on about the charity side of things. I just wanted to be honest with people, so I was…

> *I want to say thank you to the tens of thousands of people who came out and supported this. My life was very, very different four years ago. But I found running as my sanctuary. I found it was my way of being able to express myself and be who I was and not have to lie anymore. I didn't have any confidence and self-esteem and I was scared about who I was. Running gave me back my confidence, it gave me back my self-esteem. But most importantly, I'm not afraid anymore…*

Social media went ballistic, I was even trending second on Twitter – #notafraidanymore. I couldn't even remember saying it! It was insane. I was interviewed by 5 Live straight afterwards, all the papers picked up on it, and I got to see about 15 of my running club, who were in the crowd but didn't know I was going to win an award.

When I walked out of the arena with the Brownlee brothers, two of my heroes, and such focused and down-to-earth lads, people were shouting my name. Jonny turned round to me and said, with a wry smile on his face: 'Oh, it's like that now, is it?' In the following weeks, people were stopping me in the street and saying: 'Oh my God, you were that bloke on SPOTY!' I took the trophy into schools and kids were asking me for selfies and autographs. I remember handing the trophy to one of them and the look on his face was priceless, it just meant so much to him. I also lent it to Portishead Primary School for a few days. As part of the Portishead Carnival, the school put together a massive truck with 401 written on it, and paraded it through the town.

* * * * * * * * * *

Katie Russell, Ben's biggest fan: *If I hadn't found Ben when I did, I don't think I'd be the person I am today. I definitely wouldn't be at uni, and I wouldn't have been able to open up about what I've been through. I'm now such a huge believer in looking at the positives in every situation. Ben teaches us that if you do nice things for someone and listen to them, that person might go off and do the same for someone else. Maybe one day I'll be able to do for someone else what Ben did for me. He's played such a massive part in our whole family. But it's not just us, he's helped thousands of others to do things they thought they'd never do. And it's always lovely to hear everybody else's stories.*

Ben is like a little Superman – I only have to catch his eye and he knows what's going on in my head. It's spooky, as if he's got magic powers. When I have a down day, I phone Ben, we have a chat and the next day I'm ready to go again. It doesn't matter how small the issue seems, I know he'll always be there for me. Before meeting Ben, I would have just stayed in my room and cried. I didn't want to trouble people, hear people say: 'Come on, Katie, stop being silly. Forget about it, move on.' Because it wasn't silly to me, I couldn't move on. And if you get shut down, it makes you feel worse, because you think: 'Should I not have said anything? Should I not be feeling like this?' Now I know that talking to someone is so much better than holding it in. Ben taught me that it doesn't matter what you're feeling, it's never wrong.

I was super-excited to have a fresh start at uni, felt like I was ready to be my own person and live my life how I wanted to live it. On the other hand, I was worried that it wouldn't work out like that. The unknown is a bit daunting. People follow the crowd, stick together, and I wondered how I'd cope with that. But Ben also taught me that if there's something you don't want to do, or that you feel uncomfortable with, you don't have to do it. That's how you get to the good points in your life. The 401 Challenge was his way of standing up, being who he truly was and going his own way in the world. Going to uni was my way of doing the same, and I'm loving life. I've joined a bar mixology society to meet new people while learning how to make cocktails, which I'm sure will come in handy. And I've also joined the student RAG, which puts events on and fundraises for different local charities in Bristol. Remind you of anybody?!

Sarah Russell, Katie's mum: Me and my husband Alex used to joke that Katie might be with us forever, we could just never imagine her leaving home. We got her back to school and she stayed on to do her A-levels, but even then I would have bet my house that she'd never go to university – we just didn't think she'd be able to cope. She's now at university in Bristol, and that's because of the confidence and belief Ben gave her. If she doesn't want to do something, she doesn't do it. She realises that it's about people liking her for being her, not wanting her to be something else. And she's become this empathetic person. If *she senses that somebody isn't fitting in or appears left out, she looks out for them.*

I can't tell you the difference Ben has made to our lives and how much easier he's made things. Now we have our whole family back. We thought we'd lost our little girl, but Ben brought her back.

CHAPTER 15

Just The Beginning

The 401 Challenge became a bit of a movement. It made a big difference to a lot of people's lives and will always be a part of me. And to know that you've changed somebody's life for the better is a nice feeling. There are people, whose faces I don't know, who have told me over social media that running with me and taking part in the 401 gave them the confidence to do what they never thought they could. I get blamed a lot for things too – 'If it wasn't for you, I wouldn't be doing all these marathons now!' But I feel privileged to be in a position where a post on Facebook or something I say in an article or during a TV interview can have a positive effect on somebody. Ultimately, that's what humanity should be about. And there's nothing wrong with feeling good about having a positive effect on other people. People confuse it with smugness, but it's just a nice kind of pride. My mantra is: 'Make this world a little bit better than it was when you first came into it'.

. . . .

Tolu Osinnowo, 401 project manager: *I'd always cared about children's causes, but if it wasn't for the Challenge and Ben trusting me to do what I did, and telling me that I was really good at what I did, I wouldn't have had the confidence to go out there and get the job I now have with the NSPCC. I learnt from Ben that it's OK to acknowledge when you're not OK and to ask people for help. There's so* much stigma around mental health but I'm so much more open about things now, because of what Ben went through, not only as a kid but during the Challenge. He'd sometimes say to me: 'I want to give up, I can't do this anymore.' Just the thought of failure got him down. But that just taught me that it's OK to dream big and make mistakes. There are other people out there who share the same mentality and can help you along the way.

Allison Curbishley: We brought Ben up to Steve's training camp in Kielder, Northumberland, to give a talk. There were about 80–90 people in the room, ranging from very good club runners to Olympians, like Laura Weightman and Ross Murray. You could have heard a pin drop for an hour, people were hanging on his every word. That's a real skill, there aren't many people like that you come across in life. When he came down to our race, the Worcester City Run, he was treated like a superstar, especially by the women, they were flocking to him. Kyle thinks it's because they don't feel threatened, but I think it's the reverse, that they're walking away thinking: 'What a waste...'

Within the running community he has nothing but the utmost respect. Even when Ben met Laura and Ross, they were in awe of his achievements. When I introduced him to Paula [Radcliffe], Ben couldn't quite believe that she wanted to meet him. But Paula or Mo Farah, or any elite athlete, could never do what Ben did. But as soon as he finished the Challenge, the last thing he wanted to do was put his trainers on again and go for a run. You could see him spiralling down into this depression and thinking: 'What do I do now? What am I about?' He needs a major project in his life, something to plan and build from scratch, which is why I'm so glad to see *him putting all his efforts into his Foundation and motivational speaking. He's found something that he's very good at, makes him happy and a lot of other people happy. But I don't think The 401 Challenge will be the last in his life, this is just the beginning for Ben.*

You're on this planet for such a short speck of time, and I'd love to be able to leave it having touched as many people as Ben. To make a difference in the way that he has would be immense. I've made a very good friend who has hammered home the importance of living life honestly and being true to yourself. I feel so lucky to have met him. If I'm ever feeling down and I need somebody to make me laugh and tell me how it is, I'll give him a ring.

* * * * * * * * * *

It was nice to know that I'd made a difference, but five or six months after finishing the Challenge, I didn't have a job, and was thinking: 'Shit, I really need to find some money, because if I don't, I can't live.' It wasn't as if I suddenly had endorsement deals or anything. People did ask, but I wasn't in the right frame of mind to do them, and why would I endorse something I'd never used or worn? There were a lot of people who wanted to use me, which I got quite angry about. That's why Kyle became my manager, because he knows me better than anyone in the world and I trust him more than anyone in the world.

We work well as a team and he's the person who stops people taking the piss, because some people do try to. I have to charge for school visits, because I have to make a living. But I get people saying: 'We can't pay your expenses or travel, and can you do it for a big discount because we're only a small school.' And Kyle has to say: 'No, we can't.

You either want to hear his story or you don't.' That was difficult at first, because we didn't want to sound rude or uppity. But I soon realised that I was being paid for an hour of my time, paid for my life experiences. We don't live a luxurious life, but it was about recognising my own worth.

I've also started doing corporate talks, and they're interested for the same reasons as schools. There's this huge push in 'growth mindset' in corporate environments, which is basically the idea that intelligence can develop and effort leads to success. Companies are also interested in the idea of marginal gains and are constantly having to re-format their cultures, introduce new visions, new values, new goals, new strategies. I often get brought in to show their employees you can change the way you think and do things, even things you've been doing for your entire life. In other words, old dogs can learn new tricks. And doing things differently can have a positive effect. When employees hear somebody talking about all the shit they've been through in their lives and how they've managed to turn things around, that can change the way they think about how they function in a work environment. I cover so many different bases, and we're very clear that it's not necessarily about giving the client what they want. Sometimes a client doesn't even know what they want. But I'm very happy to say, touch wood, we have never had a negative corporate or school visit, and I've done 20-odd of the former and over 200 of the latter (101 of them during The 401 Challenge).

I just stand up there and bear my soul. People don't really do that and it's quite shocking for some of my audience. You might view the way I do things as winging it, but I prefer to keep things free and open, which is actually a difficult skill, or so I've been told, because there's nothing to hang onto. I know my life, and I can just pull it out when needed. I can relate to an audience better when I can keep an eye on them, and switch it up or down if need be. When I was pretending to be something I wasn't, a lot of my energy was focused on putting a face on, being something other people expected or wanted me to be. That affected a lot of things, including my ability to talk in front of people. I wouldn't have been able to talk to big groups five years ago, but the moment I accepted myself, and became happy, the confidence came, the self-esteem came, and getting up and talking to people, being open and honest, became quite empowering. I wasn't acting anymore or hiding anything, so I actually enjoy getting up on a stage and bearing my soul – it is a privilege to share my life with people.

One thing I've learnt is that while there is a natural human desire to solve people's problems, they have to do it themselves. We all want to help and give advice – 'stop doing that, this is what you should do instead' – and after the 401, I did believe I could do almost anything. But it might not be the right help and advice for that particular person, even if it was right for you. Ultimately, you don't really know what's going on in somebody's head unless they tell you, no matter how well you think you know them. During the 401, I met some people who seemed exactly like me five years ago. And people would contact me all the time, thinking I might be able to sort their lives out.

Some of the messages we had throughout the Challenge were horrific. We had parents sending us pictures of their kids that had self-harmed or been beaten up. Or they'd tell us that their son or daughter wanted to commit suicide, thinking we'd be able to do something about it. Initially, you have this outpouring of love and want to help. You end up having these deep but shallow conversations with people at the same time. You want to tell them it will get better, but you have no idea if it will. I don't know what anybody could have said to me at school to improve my situation.

The only thing that might have changed things is if Mum and Dad had removed me. All you can hope to be is a positive example. The moment you get involved in the mechanics and nitty-gritty of a particular person's problem, that's when you end up sucking your own soul dry, and you don't have any strength left to help anyone. Throughout The 401 Challenge, I had to reserve as much as I could, and it was up to Kyle and the rest of the team to shelter me from a lot of that stuff. I'm not a qualified counsellor, and just because I might have been through a similar situation doesn't mean I'm qualified to be able to deal with things like that. I could potentially be doling out the wrong advice, and something might go badly wrong.

During The 401 Challenge, I came to realise that people felt they got to know me almost personally. We had 40,000 people following us on Facebook, and if every single one of them had come to us with a problem, because they thought we had a personal relationship, I wouldn't have had time to do anything else. There were people who got quite irate about us not answering quickly, which was difficult to handle. It's nice to think that people found a measure of security or pleasure or solidarity in following my story, but there had to be a realistic expectation about how much I could give back. You want to help everybody out, but you can't. If you try, you end up killing yourself, and then you can't help anybody. That was one of the major reasons we decided to create The 401 Foundation.

We wanted to give back, and wanted to make a difference, but we couldn't do it one person at a time, we had to do it on a bigger scale. We'd discussed the idea of a 401 Foundation before, during the Challenge, but only in vague terms. The plan was to award grants to grassroots organisations and projects that focus on building confidence and self-esteem, but also tackle mental health and self-development issues. As I travelled the UK before and during the Challenge, I found a lot of communities who knew their own people better than the bigger charities did, but didn't have the money to make a difference at a local level. Not all charities are detached and impersonal, and naturally the bigger a charity gets, the more people it can help. But because government and big donors pour most of their money into those bigger charities, a lot of smaller, grassroots projects don't get a look-in. I didn't want that to be the case anymore, because I've seen first-hand how small community projects affect people in such a positive way.

During the Challenge, Scunthorpe turned out to be the biggest day, in terms of the amount of people who turned out, apart from day 401. Scunthorpe & District Athletics Club organised a pit stop at a great coffee shop, called Café Indie. It was set up by a guy who only recruited people with criminal records or mental health issues or who just couldn't get a job they really wanted. That co-operative environment built confidence in people and instilled a sense of self-worth in them. People would think: 'You know what? I might have all this shit in my past, but somebody has given me a chance, and now I have the ability to get another job and be a functioning member of society'. During my pit stop, I learned that the owner's success was also his problem, because staff would get new jobs all the time, having been given a new lease of life at the café. It was a small project but it was powerful, exactly the sort of thing we wanted to support. I don't believe it's right that if somebody has a great idea and wants to make a positive change to their community, it might fail because of a lack of money. So we wanted to be able to help these inspirational individuals. We're not going to be able to help everybody, and our grants will be between £3000–5000. But, hopefully, fingers crossed, if our financial plan for the next 10 years is accurate, we'll be able to hand out £2–3m in grants every year.

To make sure The 401 Foundation delivers what it says on the tin, we also developed an events company. I know only too well the links between running and improved mental health, so our running events are designed to build people's confidence and self-esteem. The 401 Challenge, plus The 401 Foundation, plus the events company, are all linked by this fundamental idea of trying to help people feel better about themselves.

The first event, The 401 Festival of Running, took place in Portishead in August 2017. It was a family festival of running, music and food, designed to inspire people to do things they never thought they could. There were races for kids, great bands, street-food vans, and people could do a 5k run, a 10k run or a half-marathon as part of the Festival Challenge. It was everything we wanted it to be, in terms of inclusivity and all the finer details we put into it. We had about 3000 people turn up over the two days and the feedback was immense. People loved the medals we gave out, how beautiful the location was, how supportive the locals were and how well it was organised. I was particularly pleased that they appreciated the little touches, like the mini-buses we put on to ferry people from the car park to the events village. We'll definitely be doing it again in 2018, and we hope to make it an annual fixture. The plan is to take the idea across the country – to Scotland, Wales, the North, the South-East – and hopefully, a couple of years down the line, we'll add a marathon option. In a few years, we will launch a unique running experience that will give people the chance to have their own 401 adventure. Watch this space.

When The 401 Festival of Running was over, I didn't really feel relieved, because it was a case of, 'Right, that's done, on to the next thing…' That's how my life is at the moment, there's never an opportunity to sit down and consolidate or congratulate myself on a job well done. The irony is, I've never been more challenged since I finished

The 401 Challenge. We're building a brand, which will be hard work, but I'm doing something I have a huge passion for, something that makes me happy. I'm looking forward to the next five years immensely, but I would like a little less chaos. We have an amazing board, including the chairman, Shaun Tymon, and Claude Knights, the former CEO of Kidscape. I met Shaun in Scarborough and we have become very close since, and he and the rest of our fantastic board members, including Andy Acton and Colette Fletcher, share a passion for making people's lives better. But the day-to-day running of the charity is basically all done by me. A lot of people say they'd like to help, but don't deliver when it comes to the crunch. They'll say stuff like: 'Let me know when you're ready to launch the Foundation.' I'll ring them and they'll say: 'Oh yeah, about that...' Kyle manages me, but I'm dealing with lawyers, the charity commission, councils and organising events. We have partners – companies like TrueStart Coffee, Virtual Runner UK, Nicework and EtchRock that have been with us since the start – but I have nobody working with me, and I don't make any money from The 401 Foundation. My salary comes from the various talks that I give.

. . . .

Shaun Tymon, chairman of The 401 Foundation: *I first met Ben on his second visit to Scarborough during the Challenge, in May 2016, when I ran the first of three marathons with him. I suggested he come and speak at my company's staff conference at the end of the year, which he did, and he was as inspirational as I hoped he would be. We had 260 staff, ranging from builders to accountants to solicitors, and all of them were absolutely spellbound. I think his story resonated with so many of them, because most people have felt really low* at some point in their lives and wanted to make changes, if not everyone.

He was staying with me, so I also got him to visit some schools in the Scarborough area. And although he chopped and changed his talks, there was one phrase he always used: 'Find something that makes you happy and do it every day'. I was in a bit of a dark place at the time, but I spoke to him about the problems I was having and things started to make sense. Then when he asked me to be treasurer of The 401 Foundation, that gave me a massive boost.

I'm not one for overstating things, but Ben has changed my life, no doubt about it. I've been an accountant since 1988, and accountants don't tend to make radical changes. But he made me think: 'What am I doing? Why not do something you want to do?' So I decided to take early retirement. Instead of fighting to get to the light at the end of the tunnel, Ben made me realise that I could dig myself out of the tunnel early. It was scary at first, but I'm now picking up some consultancy work, and Ben has asked me to be the chairman of The 401 Foundation, which is a dream come true. I don't get paid for it, and it takes up a lot of my time, but that's exactly what I want, because it's so exciting. Ben made me realise that if you're really passionate about something, don't wait any longer, go out and do it. Not everybody can change their circumstances completely, but almost everybody can do something that makes them happier.

When you've got someone like Ben on your side, you think you can do anything, even if you might not be sure how. I had doubts about The 401 Festival of Running, from a financial point of view, but in the end I said to Ben: 'If you think it will work, I believe it will.' And, of course, it did. Which is why I

*think The 401 Foundation will develop into the go-to charity
for self-esteem and mental health issues in the UK. We need
to generate some serious cash, and that will depend on Ben's
profile. But he just has this ability to take people with him on
his journey. It's a special talent.*

. . . .

We have plans to raise £100,000 in early 2018, through crowdfunding and Kyle is going to throw his support behind that. We will also be looking for philanthropic investment, and the aim is to become sustainable as a charity within the next two years. But crowdfunding and philanthropic investment is not going to be enough. So, the only thing for it was to start planning another challenge for 2020. Well, you didn't think I'd fall out of love with running forever? And, thankfully, The 401 Challenge didn't do any lasting physical damage, or at least nothing my chiropractor Dr. Tom Scourfield can't resolve with his magic hands. The goal is to raise more than £1m, but this time to take the challenge global. We are in the early stages of planning and will be revealing all the details very soon. But trust me, it will be worth the wait. If you thought The 401 Challenge was big, you ain't seen nothing yet.

I like the fact that The 401 Challenge had nothing to do with trying to break records or anything material, it meant there was more focus on the causes I was running for. A lot of what we learnt during The 401 – about logistics, strategy, communication – will be ploughed back into our next challenge and The 401 Foundation. Hopefully, this time the planning will run smoother, although we'll have the twin tasks of raising money for The 401 Foundation while keeping our UK audience engaged. We are planning to push the boundaries of not only endurance, but also technology, offering a direct link between the Challenge and thousands of schools throughout the UK. We're looking to be really innovative.

I still have sleepless nights, but only because my mind is so busy, thinking of all these different ideas. In 2018, we will be building The 401 Foundation team, along with all the structures required to make sure the charity's future, and the future of others, is secure.

· · · · · · · · · ·

Harry Stow, a friend for life: *I was fortunate enough to be in the audience when Ben picked up the Helen Rollason Award at the BBC Sports Personality of the Year, and I thought: 'Wow, this guy is incredible.' I'm gay, and when he finished his speech by saying, 'I'm not afraid anymore', that was a really powerful moment, because I remember feeling afraid when I first realised who I really was. I work for a county sports partnership in Hampshire, but I used to wonder if I'd always be seen as inferior within the world of sport, if people knew who I really was. But Ben made me feel like I could achieve anything.*

The fact that he was so open made me want to talk to him about what I'd been through, and he's opened a lot of doors for other people to have similar conversations, which are often difficult conversations to have. We need more role models like Ben, helping young people realise that, actually, they don't need to hide anything. I booked him for my company's awards ceremony, and afterwards he said to me: 'Why does everyone cry when I talk at events?' He doesn't realise how many people his story touches.

Ben has inspired me to be more driven, reassess my goals and test myself, because I now believe I can do more. I'm doing the London Marathon in 2018, and if there's anything I can do to help with The 401 Foundation, I want to be involved, because it's going to be such an exciting journey.

CHAPTER 16

When You Know, You Know

We were out having a meal when Kyle told me he was running the 2017 London Marathon. I'd finished the Challenge two months earlier and was having a bad week, and he wanted to cheer me up. I looked at him and said: 'Why? You hate running.' You will never get Kyle to do anything he doesn't want to do, the more you push the more he'll dig his heels in, so it's best just to leave it. Nothing in this world is impossible apart from changing his mind. But his mum and dad had done all that running with me during the Challenge – Colin ended up doing 31 marathons, while I think I've got Pat addicted to doing half-marathons – and Kyle was the only one left in the family who hadn't run one. I don't know if he felt left out, and I don't even think he did it for me. At least I hope he didn't, I hope he did it for himself.

When he announced it, I thought we'd be able to go on all these amazing runs together. People were saying: 'Oh my God, I'm so jealous, you've got the best trainer in the world!' To which Kyle responded: 'Stop right there! I'm not listening to him, I'm going to do things my way.' We went out and ran together a few times, had a lot of arguments and I decided he was right, it was best he did it on his own. To be honest, he barely trained. We did do a 16-mile run, followed by a 20-mile run the following week, when he burst into tears after 17 miles. I thought he was laughing, so started laughing at him. If anyone saw us, they would have thought I was a complete bastard. But it was genuinely difficult to tell, because he can be very blasé at times, and very dramatic at other times. He's either reclining on the floor or bouncing off the roof. But he went out and did it when it mattered.

We ran the London Marathon with our friend Hiten Vora, and some of the guys from BBC Radio 2's Children in Need Magnificent 7 project. As we were coming around the top of the Mall, we saw Paula Radcliffe, Allison Curbishley and Steve Cram and they handed Kyle this big congratulatory chocolate cake. He obviously palmed it off on me, so I was running down the Mall, carrying this great big cake, and we eventually crossed the line in 5 hours, 55 minutes. It was just so surreal. I knew he'd do it, but at the same time I was thinking: 'How the hell did he do that?' It took the piss a bit; it took me a year to run my first marathon, it took him under four months.

Kyle says he'll never do another one, but I was very proud of him. He supported me through everything I did, stuck by me during the aftermath, which couldn't have been a lot of fun for him. He's never once told me I can't do something. He has great belief in me, his standards for me are very high. During the Challenge he travelled all over the UK with me, gave up his job and his PhD to help me, and now plays a huge part in the next phase. I've had an amazing relationship with his family and their friends, from the moment we met in a Mongolian yurt (which doubled as a very nice restaurant!) in Bristol. Kyle went through some tough times, coming out as gay when he was a kid, but his relationship with his mum and dad has always been strong. But I think it's even stronger now that he's with me and you can see how proud they are of who their son is and where he is in life.

• • • • • • • • • •

Pat, Kyle's mum: *After The 401 Challenge finished, me and my friend Chez said: 'What do we do now?' People thought* we'd just stop, but I can't imagine not running now, which is kind of weird. We've done half-marathons since, lots of 10ks, and I wouldn't have done any of that without Ben. He had that effect on a lot of people, just by saying: 'Go out and do it.' If you want to do something, it might not always work, but at least give it a good go. You might start off down one path, work out it's the wrong path, take another path, and that will be the right path. Don't dwell on that wrong decision, learn from it. Kyle was originally going to do his PhD in archaeology, but he decided he didn't want to be studying it anymore, so went down a different path with Ben.

At the moment, it's all about getting Ben going with the Foundation, but Kyle also knows where he wants to go and what he wants to do. He's happy, I can see that. And that's all we hope for, for them to make a home together and for them to be happy. When Kyle first met Ben, I said to Colin: 'Can't he just find somebody with a proper job?' But Ben turned out to be far more interesting than somebody like that. People love him, absolutely love him, and he's definitely brought us all closer together.

Colin, Kyle's dad: Ben is just a very nice bloke, but also mesmerising. I'd never done a marathon before the Challenge. Not only did I do 31, but at one point I did four in seven days. I was only supposed to be driving him around, but when Kyle asked me what I was going to do while he was running, I said: 'I'm not sitting in the car all day, I'll run with him.' He also has this gift that means you can sit and listen to him all day. You don't meet many people like that in your life. He is able to convince people that they can achieve anything, and to be true to themselves. That's a great message *to be giving people, because a lot of people aren't leading lives they want to be leading.*

Ben has had a big effect on our family. For one, it costs me lots of money in trainers and running gear for Pat, rather than having to buy her new shoes. But he's changed us in other ways. After we first met Ben, me and Pat were driving down to Cornwall, and there was a phone-in on the radio, about how life should be all about doing things you never thought you'd do. I turned to Pat and said: 'I tell you something I never thought I'd do, meet my son's boyfriend and have a night out with him!' We didn't expect that to happen, but things change, and sometimes you have to move in the direction your children move in. Kyle and Ben are both strong-willed people, but they complement each other very well. Kyle accommodates Ben, and Ben does the same for Kyle. That's what happens when you meet the love of your life.

· · · · · · · · · ·

I have a loving relationship with Kyle. I can be completely me, he can be completely him, and that's the foundation of any long-lasting relationship. I don't care about holding his hand on the street or kissing him on live TV, because I'm proud of who I really am, and, for the first time in my life, I'm able to portray to the world who I really am. But neither of us sees ourselves as different from anyone else, just because we love a man. We have the most normal life together. He excites me, but also makes me frustrated and angry. He's a complex person, although I think he likes to think he's more complex than he really is. I've got him figured out now, and I don't think he likes that!

But he remains a challenge, and as you've probably worked out by now, I like a challenge. The thing I love most about him is his loyalty – I've never known anyone as loyal as him. He'll stand by me and believe in me, no matter what.

He showed a massive amount of commitment to me, right the way through the Challenge. He's not just like that with me, he's like that with all his friends. He'll put himself in the firing line for the greater good, and not many people are like that. To be fair, he's selfish at times, but he's selfless for the most part. He's a worrier, he always wants to be sorting things out. He's highly organised, which he likes to tell me a lot. He always thinks he's better than me at things, which annoys me no end, but I also love him for it. He's very impatient about certain things: if we're in the car and somebody starts talking on the radio, he'll immediately switch it over. He'll put a CD on and listen to 10 seconds of a song before turning it off and putting the radio on again. He'll fall asleep on a long journey and when we arrive home, he'll wake up and say: 'That was an easy drive, wasn't it?' But even that's endearing.

He's very picky, he'll find the smallest thing about something and write it off completely. We were looking around a house recently, and he suddenly said: 'Salmon carpets. Don't like it.' I obviously said: 'But we can change the carpets.' And he said: 'I'm not living in a house with salmon carpets...' And that was that. His language can be very dramatic and expressive and he exaggerates a lot. He'll come in the house and say: 'Oh. My. God. It took me four hours to get to Bristol.' And I'll be like: 'So, half an hour then?' But that's just something else I love about him. And, of course, I find him devastatingly attractive. All of which is why I asked him to marry me.

Some people think it's really fast. They ask me: 'How did you know?' I just do. Saying it was the next logical step makes it sound very unemotional, but it was really. And he kept asking when I was going to propose. Kyle's about as subtle as a brick. But I love him, he's the man I want to be with for the rest of my life, and to say that in front of other people is important to me. I'd been planning the proposal for five months. He always wanted to go to New York, and I love the place. So I went and asked his mum and dad for permission, booked up the trip, and got a number of people on board from his work, because obviously he'd need some time off. I also had to have a word with his hairdresser, to coax him in, because he always said he wanted to look good when I asked him. In all, I got about 50 people involved. Everything was carefully stage-managed, but I decided to do it earlier than originally planned, because I wanted everybody who had been involved to be surprised.

A lot of people have asked how a marriage proposal works in a gay relationship. It's like with any relationship: one person asks and the other person hopefully says yes. I put the plane tickets in a brown envelope and gave them to him in our living room. When he opened the envelope, he couldn't read what it said. Things never happen like they do in the movies. He said: 'What's this?' I said: 'For God's sake, read it! It's tickets to New York!' He said: 'Why are we going to New York?' I said: 'Because I'd like you to marry me…' He started wandering all over the flat, picking things up and putting them down again in random places. He just didn't know what to do with himself. That only lasted so long. Within about an hour and a half of proposing, the whole guest list was sorted.

· · · · · · · · · ·

Kyle Waters, Ben's partner: *I knew something was going on, because Ben was acting a bit weird. And I kept asking* *people questions and they kept just smiling at me. But I was still quite shocked when he proposed. He had to ask me: 'Is that a yes?!' And I said: 'Get down on one knee and ask me again...' He did, I said yes and he started crying. I was a bit annoyed that about 50 people knew about it and I didn't have a clue, but I knew I was going to marry him within a month of meeting him. It might sound corny, but when you know, you know.*

I'd had a few boyfriends before, but Ben was something completely different. There are only certain people who can put up with me, and he's one of them. What do I love about Ben? Everything. Ben is just Ben, and that's why everyone loves him. He's just such a genuine person and will give time to anybody. He's a strong, confident character who sees the best in people. He likes to give people more than two chances, which I definitely don't. He's just a lovely, genuine, caring guy who wants to do something good in the world. He's made me a better person, in part because I want to be a better person for him (although I feel the need to add that I don't think he could have done what he's done without me!). I should have quit archaeology years ago, because being a PA is something I'm really good at. I knew I was capable in that field, but it was Ben who made me act on it. That's what Ben does for lots of people, makes them realise what they can achieve in life. He's shown that you can do anything if you put your mind to it, even in the face of adversity. Don't let anybody tell you that you can't do something, because you can.

I knew Ben would finish the Challenge, even when his back went. Because of his stubbornness, he's able to do absolutely anything. Running 401 marathons had a worse

*effect on his mental state than his physical state, but I was
never really worried about him. There were times when
things almost got on top of him, but I always knew he'd be
strong enough to get through it. And if anything went wrong,
I'd just sort it all out, because he didn't need any added
stress. I'm literally the most organised person in the world,
and I wasn't going to take any shit from anybody, because
all I was worried about was making sure he completed the
Challenge.*

*He lost his drive after the 401, and I found his depression
difficult to relate to because I've never suffered with it. But
I wanted to be a better person for him, so adapted and
helped him through it. He's a very inwards person, whereas
I'm quite verbal – if something is pissing me off I'll have a
rant. He's the constant in the relationship (apart from that
period after the Challenge), whereas I'm more up and
down. But he's certainly more up and down than he was,
because of the Foundation and Festival of Running and
everything else he's doing now, and the fact he's doing it
all on his own. I do think he takes on too much, but until
we get investors, he's not going to be able to employ
anyone to help him out. But if anyone can do it on his own,
it's Ben.*

*I try to steer him away from being a gay role model,
because I don't think his sexuality had anything to do with The* ·
*401 Challenge. He does embrace his sexuality, but I don't
think it should be a defining part of his story. He's a normal
bloke, and 'normal' to me is about embracing everybody,
whether they're gay or straight or whatever. When I say he's
a normal bloke, I'm aware that to other people he's amazing.
I know he's amazing, but I also know the real Ben. I see him*

when he's being a little shit, when he's having a meltdown or stressing about stuff or wound up or angry. He doesn't show that side of himself to other people. It's almost like he's become a celebrity of sorts, in that he can't truly be himself in public. I enjoy going to things like Pride of Britain and SPOTY. But he'll never think of himself as a celebrity or put himself on a pedestal, he'll always just see himself as Ben. Sometimes I say to him: 'Ben, you are inspirational, that's why they're giving you this award.' He forgets how special he is.

* * * * * * * * * *

We had a phenomenal time in New York, walking miles, doing all the usual touristy stuff. It's not like I felt I had to give him something in exchange for what he'd done for me, it wasn't a tit-for-tat thing, but I wanted him to know how much I valued him as the love of my life and my soulmate. For so many years, I never thought it would be something I'd do. I was resigned to living that life that I had before. Five years ago, I'd be driving into Portishead, fantasising about what my life would be like if I was an openly gay man. Never in my wildest dreams did I think I could have anything like I have now, because that's not what I thought gay people could have. I thought being gay was to be ostracised, to be different, to be unhappy in life. But I feel like I have the luckiest life in the world. I'm leading what I can only describe as the most normal life I've ever lived, and those days of doubt seem so far away. That's one hell of a five-year plan.

We've found a wedding venue but it's booked out for 2018, so we're looking at September 2019. We've decided we don't want kids, so we're going to get two dogs instead – a Labrador and a Border Terrier. I'd like to buy our own home. Other than that, I don't really know what married life will look like. I just know it will be happy and challenging, for me and for Kyle. So far, my life with him has lived up to how I imagined it would be on those drives. It's exactly how I wished it would be, as if all my dreams have come true.

CHAPTER 17

A Nice Place To Be

It frustrates me when people say: 'I can't do that.' Everybody has something incredible inside of them, they just have to find out what it is. I could have quite easily stayed in that job that was draining my soul, chasing those big bucks, living in that big house, driving that big car, paying into that pension plan, taking those two holidays a year I was too stressed to enjoy, but I chose to get rid of it all, because my happiness was worth more to me than all of it. It's all about creating your own version of success, not adhering to what society tells you success looks like. It took me a long, long time to work that out, and it was bloody hard at times, because some of the choices I made were uncomfortable. I found happiness eventually, but only after a long, hard slog.

When you're on holiday, you'll always hear people say: 'I'm dreading going back to work.' Obviously, that means they're not happy at work. But they'll go back anyway, moan about it for the next six months, before going on holiday again. And then they'll spend the last few days of that holiday moaning about having to go back to work again. You hear it all the time in the corporate world: 'Find out what makes you happy!' They're right when they say that, but hardly anybody does. It takes guts, and so many of us have lost our adventurous spirit, our ability to dream. That's why far too few people find out what makes them truly happy. We're all a bit like lemmings, eager to please, following everybody else, so that many of us end up falling off a cliff. The key is taking steps to change your situation. I used to have moments when I was pretending to be something I wasn't, when

I'd say: 'I wish I could do this, I wish I could do that.' And I'd never actually do it. But I don't think like that anymore because I made a life to fit me, rather than trying to squeeze myself into an ill-fitting life. If anything, my life has gone too crazy. I wake up every morning thinking: 'Why don't we do this? Why don't we do that?' I have so many ideas whirring around my head that I can't keep up with them. But better to create your own crazy life than have an unhappy life created for you.

I'm not going to sit here and claim I don't wish for material things. It's nice to have a nice car and a nice house, and wanting those things doesn't make you a bad person. I want a nice car and a nice house one day, and I'd like to earn decent money, but not if it means changing who I am. The problem is when you start to change who you are and how you live your life because the love of material things starts to override everything else. That's why money is not the be-all and end-all for me, because my happiness trumps everything. It's good to have money, because it gives you plenty of opportunities to do certain things, especially in terms of building new projects. But I'm not going to do anything I don't want to do, just to bring money in. That's the difference.

All the way through The 401 Challenge, people would say to me: 'Are you going to write a book?' And I'd say: 'Why would I? I don't read books, let alone write them.' I thought it would be a bit hypocritical of me. But the more and more people asked, the more and more I started to think: 'Maybe there's something in this.' I started to realise why they were asking, because the project had such a profound effect on people's lives. Talking to people about my experiences has made me realise I've made a genuine difference. I have that realisation every day, therefore I'm happy. People often say to me: 'It must be amazing to have your life.' And I say: 'You can, if you want it enough.' I want people to feel what I feel, ignite lots of fires in lots of bellies.

It might sound absurd, given that I've written a book, but I've never been one to dwell on the past. Would I have attempted The 401 Challenge if the things that happened to me as a kid hadn't happened? Maybe, but probably not. I wouldn't wish what I went through on anybody, and I'm certainly not grateful for it. I used to be angry with my parents for sending me to boarding school, but not anymore. The reality is it made me the person I am today. And maybe if those things hadn't happened, I'd have ended up working in an office for the rest of my life and absolutely loving it. I don't even regret the time I spent working in an office. The people I worked with in my previous careers were amazing and a lot of the skills I learnt there I now use in creating The 401 Foundation. I honestly believe that without that time I spent in my old jobs, I wouldn't have been able to do what I'm doing now. You have to pluck the positives from everything. But if you're not loving life – and the elephant in lots of living rooms across the land is happiness or contentment – it's about changing the situation you find yourself in. It was me who decided I wasn't going to let the past affect me anymore. It was me who decided to change and get the help I needed to do that. It was me who decided to get rid of the money and material things and figure out what made me happy. It was me who decided to start running, with some prompting from a friend. It was me who decided to do all of the things I did that brought me to the place I am now. Most people have the ability to do what they want, when they want to do it, but not many people do anything about it. If you live your life always thinking about ifs, buts and maybes, you're not really living. None of that stuff matters, all that matters to me is that I'm now in a situation where I can make a change in people's lives, and that's a nice place to be.

I don't have the time to think about what life might have been like had I not rolled the dice. I don't really have much emotional attachment to the past anymore, and I have no memory of the pain. It's been washed away, it doesn't even feel like it is a part of my life. While I was doing the Challenge, a few people from school got in touch to say: 'Was I one of the bullies? If so, I'm really sorry.' None of them were. But I honestly don't think I'd be that bothered if I bumped into any of them. I don't honestly know why they did what they did to me, whether it was low self-esteem or jealousy or whatever. But they're so removed from my life now it's irrelevant because I've dealt with what they put me through, run the anger out of me. It was running that allowed me to get rid of all my negative emotions. When I first started running, I was still affected by what had happened to me. I'd tried to flush it away, but it had started to bubble up again. But running gave me an outlet, allowed me to cut the ties to the past and drift off to a better place, where I could be me. I felt free, as if I didn't have a care in the world. And the more I ran – and I ran quite a bit – the more time I had to file away all that shit that happened to me. I used to hear people talking about Zen and think it was a load of bollocks, but I now think there's some truth in it, because I think I found it.

It took blood, sweat and tears to complete The 401 Challenge, and there were lots of tough days. But there were also lots of phenomenal moments. It was like a therapeutic journey, instances from my life would suddenly come back to me – I'd be running in the Highlands and I'd have a memory of when I was at school. But the fact that those memories no longer had an adverse effect on me confirmed that I'd already dealt with them and changed as a person. I needed to have dealt with all that stuff before I started the Challenge, otherwise I would have been doing it for very different reasons, and probably for the wrong ones.

Telling a story about the past and letting the past affect how you feel now are two different things. I don't let my past define me, but I use my past in a positive way, to make a difference. People might say that I'm burying it, but that's just nonsense: filing is very different to burying. I've come across a lot of amateur psychologists, well-meaning people, I hope, but people who assume they know more about me than myself. But I know me and I know what covering things up looks and feels like. People sometimes say to me: 'Oh my God, you had such a tough childhood, that must really affect you?' And I say: 'No, it doesn't.' And they say: 'Oh. Have you not dealt with it yet?' And I'll be thinking: 'Yes, I really have!'

* * * * * * * * * *

Dan Smith, Ben's brother: *Bullying certainly affected me adversely, but because Ben was bullied far worse and for longer, it did him more damage. I played a lot of sport growing up, and when I decided to focus on rugby, my confidence grew. I left boarding school, went to a day school and was able to make a fresh start and forge my own identity. When I was 16, I got a rugby scholarship to a private school in Bristol, before signing for Bath Rugby, when I was 18. Meanwhile, Ben was struggling at university. I remember him unpacking his bags in Middlesbrough, and getting that same feeling in my gut as when he packed for boarding school. For most of our late teens and 20s, we lived very different lives. There were glimpses of our old relationship, but it just wasn't the same. We didn't really know how to be brothers any more. When I left Bath Rugby, I signed for Rotherham Titans and then Doncaster Knights, around the same time as Ben moved down to Bristol. If he needed me, I was there for him, but neither of us made much of an effort.*

When Ben came out as gay, he changed as a person. He became happier and more confident, and it was at that point that we tried to rebuild a relationship. When I heard he was going to run 401 marathons in 401 days, I thought: 'You know what, he'll do it. It's so off the wall and no-one will expect him to complete it, so he will.' He grew in confidence as the Challenge progressed, and I believe it was therapeutic and cathartic for him, and he exorcised some demons along the way. But it's only recently that Ben and I have sat down and properly talked, and it's Kyle and my beautiful wife Sarah that have helped bring us back together. Sarah is the most amazing woman I have ever known, has changed my life beyond recognition and challenged me to face my own demons. Kyle has done just the same for Ben. Ben and I have had brutally honest talks about the past, and this has transformed our relationship for the better. Through the support of Kyle and Sarah, I have got my big brother back, and Ben has got his little brother back, and I'm incredibly grateful.

Recently, Sarah and I became parents to our beautiful boy Bob. He is the most incredible little man, the love we have for him can't be put into words. And parenthood has made me appreciate just how great a job my mum and dad did, and continue to do. They didn't get it right all the time, but I can see now that everything they did for us was out of love. Thank you Mum and Dad, for everything.

* * * * * * * * * *

I used to fear what people would think if I opened up, but that's changed. These days I have a different perspective on life, and I don't really care what people think based on what I say about my past. Talking about stuff has become almost a compulsion, because look where *not* talking about stuff got me. I've now shared my story with people in the UK and around the world, most of them complete strangers, which is both weird and strangely liberating. You open yourself up to people and they either accept you or they don't. As soon as you become comfortable with that, you can talk about almost anything. Not everybody is open to hearing about what happened to me. Some people want to stay in one place and live a rigid life, and don't even want to hear about alternative possibilities. But I believe we're in this world to experience as much as we can and interact with as many people as possible. Whatever your life looks like, that isn't the way it has to be forever, just because it's how it's always been. It isn't the way it has to be forever, just because that's what you were taught from childhood. It isn't the way it has to be forever, just because you've got a well-paid job and a family. Are you doing what you really want to do? Is doing what you're doing making you happy or content? Really happy? Happy in your soul? As happy as you could be?

That said, writing this book was always going to be a challenge because nobody has ever heard the full version in one go. But maybe this book was the final push I needed to clear up any lingering issues. Writing it dredged a few things up, things I thought had disappeared forever. The puzzle wasn't complete, there were still bits jumbled up or missing, but the process was more cathartic than troubling. I wouldn't go as far as to say there are bits of the old me left over, but certain things still affect me. There are things that frustrate me and make me nervous. Things still worry me, just in a different way. I get anxious about the Foundation because of a constant need to put myself under pressure and strive for perfection. Everything has to be done right first time, and the thought that something might not be gets my heart thumping through my chest again. No doubt that stems from my experiences at school, but at least now I'm channelling those feelings into something positive. If I hear that somebody has said something bad about me or I sense that they don't quite get who I am, that stings. Before The 401 Festival of Running, we received a complaint from a local resident, who said she hoped it wouldn't be a success and become an annual event because it would cause chaos for Portishead. That really got to me because I'd put my heart and soul into trying to do something positive for the community. It didn't matter that we'd had literally thousands of positive comments, that one negative comment drowned everything else out. I hated the fact that she'd had that effect on me.

Like most people, I get stressed when I have lots of stuff on my mind, and I still sometimes lack confidence and self-esteem. I'll end up in situations, such as when I hid in the toilet at the Australian High Commission, where I was thinking: 'I shouldn't be here.' I regress, feel like I used to, hiding from the bullies at school. Get me running and all my barriers come down; I'm as open as anything, will talk to anybody and just be me but stick me in a posh social function and I wither and die. I loved the fact I was invited to meet the Queen at Buckingham Palace and the Prime Minister at 10 Downing Street, but I find all the small talk that comes with those things a bit awkward.

When I first started doing visits to very posh schools, I felt extremely uncomfortable because they reminded me of my school. It wasn't the schools' fault, I just had this feeling inside me that I wasn't good enough to be there. My boarding school was a cruel environment, but I know it's not anymore. After I finished The 401 Challenge, a radio station rang me up and said: 'Could you come on the programme and talk about how much you're against boarding schools?' I said: 'What makes you think I am?' They just assumed I was. But a lot of boarding schools, including mine, have changed for the better and now have world-class pastoral care systems in place. Not all schools are like that. Sometimes, when kids move from primary to secondary school, their education stops being pastoral and holistic and becomes more focused on results. Nowadays, schools have to be run as businesses, I get that, but if that has a detrimental effect on kids' confidence and self-esteem, it doesn't really matter what grades they get, they'll struggle in life. I wouldn't send my kids to boarding school, but not because of what happened to me. Some kids thrive in that environment, but I'd just want my own at home with me. Then again, people always say, 'I'd never do this, I'd never do that', but it's not always that simple. Parents want what's best for their kids, but circumstances change, just as my parents' circumstances changed.

Sometimes I wake up in the morning and think: 'My God, everything's going so well – when am I going to get the call or text or email telling me it's all gone to shit again?!' But even that's part of the joy of where I am in my life right now. I'm trying to create new things all the time, which is fun and exciting, but also means lots of things will go wrong. But failure is a privilege of those who try. Life doesn't always go to plan, and the true test of your character and personality is how you react when that happens. I've already proved to myself that when things get tough – at school, at university, during my marriage and divorce, during The 401 Challenge – I can manage. And having battled through all that darkness, nothing can ever be as bad again.

There were a lot of times during The 401 Challenge when I thought: 'What on earth am I doing?' But the project was like one gigantic tribute to the thing that made everything possible. Five years ago, my life was this murky mess. Running was like a purifying tablet: as soon as it was dropped into the mix, things started to become clearer. Eventually, I ran so much, all the murkiness was gone. And that's what I wanted other people to experience. The fact I'm not a professional athlete carried weight. I still honestly don't know if there's anything special about me or not. Maybe I do have the gift of stubbornness or persistence, but I still had to go looking for them. And if you do take the view that what I did was special, then by extension everybody has something special inside of them, because I'm still just a normal bloke.

The moment you find that thing that makes you happy or content, everything else falls into place. I tell kids that the most important thing in life is finding inner happiness, not just in the head, but also in the heart. Too many of us are ruled by the head and don't listen to our hearts enough. There are so many metaphors I could use for how running was the key to my contentment. As well as a purifying tablet, it was like my WD-40. I'd been rusting away, but running freed things up again. For so long, I thought that almost everybody was bad and out to get me. But running, and by extension, The 401 Challenge, made me realise that most people are essentially good. Running made me realise that anything is possible. Things we haven't done, we just haven't figured out how to do them yet. Running gave me the confidence to be who I truly am and live the life I wanted to live. Your gifts might be different to mine and you might not fancy running 401 marathons in 401 days but there will be a song inside you, if only you look.